Social Issues

A Bishop's Perspective

Emerson S. Colaw

DISCIPLESHIP RESOURCES
MATERIALS FOR GROWTH IN CHRISTIAN FAITH AND LIFE
P.O. Box 189 • Nashville, TN 37202 • Phone (615) 340-7284

Unless otherwise indicated, all scripture quotations are taken from the New Revised Standard Version of the Holy Bible, Copyright © 1989 by The Division of Christian Education of the National Council of the Churches of Christ in the U.S.A. and used by permission.

Cover design by Donna Richmond.

Cover transparencies courtesy of John Cummings.

ISBN 0-88177-101-5

Library of Congress Card Catalog Number: 90-84524

DR101B

Contents

Introduction

In 1908, The Methodist Church adopted an affirmation of social principles that was entitled "The Methodist Social Creed." It was an effort to define how the Methodist people ought to act in relation to a changing society. With minimal alteration this statement remained a part of our heritage until The Methodist Church merged with The Evangelical United Brethren Church in 1968. With the union came a document titled "Basic Beliefs regarding Social Issues and Moral Standards of the E.U.B. Church." Because there were differences between the statement of The Methodist Church and that of The Evangelical United Brethren, a Quadrennial Study Commission was authorized to produce a new set of social principles. These were adopted by the 1972 General Conference and printed in *The Book of Discipline*. With some alteration, they have continued to the present day.

Many of us understand the story of a boy who brought home a report card indicating a poor grade in conduct. His explanation and defense was, "Conduct is my hardest subject." And so it is with us. In this complex and confusing world, however, it is not only hard to do right, it is also difficult to know what is right. We may wish for a rule book, but, unfortunately, we are faced with ever-changing issues and situations. That is why this book is offered.

It should be noted, as we examine statements from the Social Principles of the church, that our aim will not be to mandate simplistic solutions. That would be foolish. United Methodists are diverse. We come from a variety of traditions and look at issues from diverse perspectives. The Social Principles themselves are the result of open debate and compromise on the floor of our General Conference. And every four years the principles are open again to discussion and reformulation. These principles do, however, represent the collective wisdom (from scripture, tradition, experience, and reason) of the people called United Methodist at this point in history. As such, they can be and are very helpful in untangling the web of issues we are called to address.

I am particularly eager to say a word to those who are new

members in The United Methodist Church. Every denomination
has tradition, historic convictions, and points of view that charac-
terize its life, and this includes The United Methodist Church. John
Wesley said, "Faith and good works belong together." The early
Methodist preachers in the United States rallied under the banner,
"Spread Scriptural Holiness and Reform the Continent." Speaking
out on important issues is one of the things that makes us United
Methodists. New members will wish to know the beliefs of the
church as these inform significant contemporary problems and
concerns.

The 1988 *Discipline* says: "The Social Principles are a prayerful
and thoughtful effort on the part of the General Conference to
speak to the human issues in the contemporary world from a
sound biblical and theological foundation as historically demonstrated in United Methodist traditions. They are intended to be
instructive and persuasive in the best of the prophetic spirit. The
Social Principles are a call to all members of The United Methodist
Church to a prayerful, studied dialogue of faith and practice."[1]
This book is designed to be a resource as the reader responds to
this call.

1

Ecology

On September 27, 1962, Rachel Carson published *Silent Spring*. Shortly before publication she told a friend that, while she might have helped the environment a little, "it would be unrealistic to believe one book could bring complete change." The book did not bring complete change. It did begin a process of making the American people sensitive to an emerging crisis. The book was not gloomy, but it was a warning. It also offered specific directions, ingenious and full of hope, on how humans could change their ways. She died April 14, 1964. The U.S. Secretary of the Interior, Stewart L. Udall, was one of her pallbearers. Prince Philip sent the biggest wreath. And her book did change the mindset of a people and a planet. Today ecological issues are routinely listed along with peace concerns as the top challenges confronting not only the American people but the world. And Rachel Carson was one of the standard bearers!

Since she wrote her book, our sense of urgency has deepened. The great Alaskan oil spill at Valdez in 1989 and the Persian Gulf spill in 1991 dismayed and frightened the entire world. We are all keenly aware of our dependence upon oil, yet these spills dramatized our inability to control the drilling and transportation of it. There were daily newscasts showing the fish and ducks and sea animals dying in the gunk. The pristine beaches and waves were greasy black. The spills were ecologically and economically disastrous.

Every time some ecosystem is destroyed, it affects people around the world. Genesis tells us God created the earth, saw that it was good, then made man and woman and put them in a "garden in Eden." Adam and Eve were given responsibility for this garden. But a crisis has developed in Eden. We live in a world of vanishing beauty, of shrinking open space, and of an overall environment that is diminished daily by pollution, noise, and blight.

Travelers in space say it is easy to spot Los Angeles by observing the large blanket of smog hovering over it. Throughout our land, oxygen-producing fields, forests, and meadows are being de-

1

voured by highways, shopping centers, and urban subdivisions at a rate of over 3,000 acres a day!

Furthermore, the Public Health Service estimates that in a typical year we throw away more than 600 pounds of paper per person, 240 cans, and 130 bottles or jars. Thirty million junk cars litter our landscape and that is augmented by 100 million discarded tires. Most major cities simply do not know what they will do with their trash in the near future. Garbage has literally backed up in the streets, supermarkets have taken to guarding their dumpsters, and Goodwill Industries reports that half of the "contributions" to its collection boxes have been garbage—real garbage.

Industry releases into the air every year more than three billion pounds of thirty-six chemicals suspected of causing cancer and other chronic diseases. Half of the drinking water supply systems of major cities draw on ground water that contains toxic chemicals. The daily newspaper has made us aware of the expected warming of the earth from industrial gases accumulating in the atmosphere, the negative impact of deforestation, the poisoning of our lakes and oceans with industrial effluents, and the excessive use of pesticides. Solutions to these problems will require all our Christian wisdom and insight.

One of my vivid childhood memories is that of living through the dust bowl era of Kansas in the early Thirties. For days we did not see the sun as the air was filled with dust. Fence rows were drifted over. This was the result of the fact that during World War I, when the United States needed to help feed other parts of the world, thousands of acres of prairie were ploughed under so wheat could be grown. Fifteen years later a price was paid for the abuse of the land. The years of the dust storms were a frightful time. Isaiah 24:5-6 says: "The earth lies polluted under its inhabitants; for they have transgressed the laws, violated the statutes, broken the everlasting covenant. Therefore a curse devours the earth, and its inhabitants suffer for their guilt." These ominous words suggest what happens when the laws of nature are violated. The inhabitants of the land suffer.

A person cannot go without air for more than six minutes without suffering some degree of brain damage. We know that, yet we put more than 140 million tons of pollutants into the air each year, threatening the ozone and placing in jeopardy the future of all living things.

Water is an essential. This water planet depends on the sea for survival. If nations continue polluting the oceans with oil slicks and chemical wastes, the sea will die and with it all human life. For many years I spent a portion of each summer at Lake Erie. It was tragic to watch Lake Erie dying from a discharge of industrial poison at the rate of a ton per minute. Fortunately, in the Seventies, corrective action was taken and the lake is well on the way to being restored. But unless remedial action had been taken, it would have ended up as a fetid swamp.

Every eight seconds a new American is born. This infant is a disarming little thing who begins to scream loudly in a voice that can be heard for seventy years or more. This baby is screaming for 56 million gallons of water, 21,000 gallons of gasoline, 10,000 pounds of meat, 28,000 pounds of milk and cream. Americans are prodigious consumers. With only 6 percent of the world's population, we use one-third of its energy. As soon as our new baby is born, it makes contact with our throw-away society. Diapers are disposable. Formula bottles are disposable. The infant is dusted with powder from throw-away plastic bottles and cleaned with moistened paper towels in plastic containers. But all of us know that the earth's resources are finite. If population, pollution, and consumption continue to grow at present rates, there will be a disastrous collapse in a few decades.

For this reason the 1988 General Conference adopted a rather lengthy passage dealing with the natural world. Now part of the Social Principles, the statement begins:

> All creation is the Lord's and we are responsible for the ways in which we use and abuse it. Water, air, soil, minerals, energy resources, plants, animal life, and space are to be valued and conserved because they are God's creation and not solely because they are useful to human beings. Therefore, we repent of our devastation of the physical and nonhuman world. Further, we recognize the responsibility of the church toward life style and systemic changes in society that will promote a more ecologically just world and a better quality of life for all creation.[2]

The resolution then goes on to detail some of the ways in which we are to care for the natural world, conserve energy, protect the life and health of animals, and bring a high sense of respect to space exploration.

This concern is based in biblical teaching. In Genesis 2:15 we read, "The Lord God took the man and put him in the garden of Eden to till it and keep it." Psalm 24:1 says, "The earth is the Lord's and all that is in it, the world, and those who live in it." Paul writes, "You reap whatever you sow" (Gal. 6:7). In Jeremiah 2:7 there is this word from the Lord: "I brought you into a plentiful land to eat its fruits and its good things. But when you entered you defiled my land."

Our hymnody reflects our sense of praise and gratitude for God's creation. Maltbie Babcock wrote: "This is my Father's world, and to my listening ears all nature sings, and round me rings the music of the spheres. This is my Father's world: I rest me in the thought of rocks and tress, of skies and seas; his hand the wonders wrought."

Scripture also reminds us, "From everyone to whom much has been given, much will be required" (Luke 12:48). God has indeed shed grace upon United Methodists and all others in the United States, but along with the gifts comes responsibility. Let's examine this within the frame work of three words: *sanctification, shalom,* and *stewardship.*

Sanctification

Wes Granberg-Michaelson, writing in *Sojourners* (October 24, 1982), calls for a theology of global sanctification. He says that as redemption is to promote the work of sanctification in our lives, and thus transform our lives into the life of Christ, so the redemption of creation should sanctify the earth, which means it will be transformed through the sovereignty of Christ. What does it mean to promote works of sanctifying the earth? We sanctify the earth when we revere it in the sense that we stand in awe before it and draw illumination, wisdom, truth, and inspiration from it. As someone has said, "Life is not so much a problem to be solved but a mystery to be revered." Creation can provide "patches of God-light" in the woods of our experience, glimmerings of divine handiwork that help us to gather our spiritual bearings. This is not pantheism, that is, the idea that somehow God and nature are the same. It is rather the biblical affirmation that the heavens declare the glory of God. Paul says in Romans, "Ever since the creation of the world his eternal power and divine nature, invisible though they are, have been understood and seen through the things he has made" (1:20). As I indicated earlier, I was reared on a farm. As we did battle with flood and drought, heat and cold, trying to wrest a livelihood from the soil, there was little time for sentiment. Life was too stern for that. Yet there was an appreciation, a reverence born out of an awareness that our lives did depend upon our care of the good earth.

Perhaps you have visited the famed Callaway Gardens near Atlanta, Georgia. As you enter, there is a sign which says, "Remove nothing from the gardens except nourishment for the soul, consolation for the heart, inspiration for the mind." Composers such as Beethoven, Debussy, Vaughan Williams, and many others have created music that reflects the wonder of nature. Poets in this country, namely Walt Whitman, Henry David Thoreau, William

Cullen Bryant, among a long list, have expressed the inspiration they received from nature. There is a Persian fable that says: "If of thy mortal goods thou art bereft, and from thy slender store two loaves alone to thee are left; sell one, and with the dole, buy hyacinths to feed the soul." The sanctification of nature begins with a sense of awe and wonder.

While I was serving as bishop in Minnesota, one of our superintendents, James Schneider, was a poet and mystic as well as an effective superintendent. He would often remind the other superintendents and me of the transcendent when we were bogged down with the dailiness of the task. Among his personal writings:

> We dare not overlook the pleasure of touching nature ourselves. To taste it, to smell it, to look at it, to listen to it, not with clever devices, but with ourselves, our own alive devices. As we learn to touch nature directly, reverently, and with joy, we will develop the nearly lost art of wonder. In our cherished sophistication we are almost ashamed to stand amazed, awed, or puzzled before something beautiful and created. We hesitate to enjoy unless we can first explain. The ancient psalmist knew well the importance of wonder and awe. "O come, let us worship and bow down."

I have heard parishioners say they could worship God on the golf course as well as in church. The appropriate rejoinder is: "But you don't." Still, there is a sense in which the affairs of contemporary life are put in proper perspective when we see them in the light of God's creation. The vastness of creation quietly humbles one's spirit. Creation-centered spirituality is a healthy and wholesome way of approaching life. Natural beauty stirs us to rise above ourselves. The touch of beauty, when we feel it, is not to be merely a passing delight; it is the call of God, inviting us to turn to God.

Unfortunately, it is doubtful that Christians have been any more thoughtful in the care of the earth than non-Christians. The "Christian West" has exploited natural resources more than any other part of the world simply because we have the technological resources to do so. The time is obviously here for an attitude of sanctification in our approach to the earth.

Shalom

Our call to earthkeeping and our perspectives on the global environmental crisis are further illuminated by the biblical concept of *shalom*. As usually translated, this Hebrew word appears in the Bible as "peace." But its meaning is richer than the absence of war. It means a state of wholeness. It means humanity living in proper relationship to the creation. *Respect* is a key word.

We have often used Genesis 1:26, with its admonition to have dominion, as a license to seize the land for selfish purposes, to rule over creation. We have manipulated, controlled, altered our environment, and exploited earth's abundant riches. But the time has come to see nature not as an environment to be conquered but as a partner, a colleague.

This requires the ability to say "enough." What do we really want from life? Most of us want the right to eat well, breathe clean air, have decent housing, enjoy natural beauty, experience silence, be protected from pesticide poisoning, be free from nuclear war, educate our children, and have grandchildren. A Harris poll asked a cross section of Americans what they wanted most. After "time with family," the answers were in this order: green grass and trees around me, neighbors with whom I feel comfortable, a church of my faith nearby, a first-rate shopping area, and schools for my children. But in order to have this, we must learn the restraint of saying "enough." We must learn to emphasize the quality of life rather than its quantity. We must encourage those enjoyments that do not use up resources or pollute the environment. We are partners with nature. This may require an asceticism that depends not upon withdrawing from the world but upon searching for new ways of acting in the world. For example, several of our United Methodist general boards and agencies have adopted a policy that they will not use the traditional Styrofoam coffee cups at their meetings because they are not biodegradable.

Technology has vastly improved our standard of living, if not the quality of our lives. Take a look at the good old days of 150 years ago. Life expectancy for men was thirty-eight years, women less. The workweek was seventy-two hours. Food was monotonous and scarce. In the winter you froze and in the summer you sweltered. When the epidemic came—as it did about every year—it would probably carry off someone in your family. You would probably never hear the sound of an orchestra, own very many books, or travel more than twenty miles from the place you were born.

But technology is hurrying us into the future faster than our institutions can cope with it, and we must develop a theology adequate for the time. Albert Schweitzer once said we need to develop a reverence for life that includes a recognition that air, earth, and water have a life of their own and must be respected. We speak of the rape of the land. When abusing nature, we are violating a personality. We must not think of nature as an "it" but a "thou."

Thirteenth-century monks held a respectful attitude toward nature. St. Francis recognized the spiritual autonomy of all parts of nature and spoke of Brother Sun, Sister Moon, Brother Wind, and Sister Earth, each of whom praised the Creator in his or her own way. St. Francis is the patron saint of ecology. Shalom comes as we live in partnership. In a valid marriage, the partners cherish and respect each other. To cherish and respect nature is to preserve God's shalom.

A New Ethic of Frugality

The United States has been blessed with an abundant supply of cheap energy. Even in a day when oil is not as plentiful as it once was and we import more than half the oil we use, still other Western nations pay twice as much or more for their gasoline as we do. But our lifestyle, and our nation, was built on a plentiful supply of energy.

In the old feudal state, a few at the top had privilege and the good life, but the masses were illiterate, lived in grinding poverty with little hope for improvement. The Age of Enlightenment, the Industrial Revolution, and the Reformation changed all of that. There was theological talk of the "priesthood of all believers." Every person was precious in the sight of God. Universities were born, frontiers conquered, expectations lifted. Cheap energy created problems, but it also offered opportunities. It created a civilization—the one we now enjoy. Some say we have not used our cheap energy wisely. There have been mistakes, but it has not been all wrong.

Is the huge, interconnected power grid that covers the continental United States some sort of blunder? Were we foolish to build the great net of highways that made us a more unified people? Is the industrial might of this nation a gross mistake, one we should have passed by for the simpler, agricultural existence of the nineteenth century? Were our farmers deluded in using energy as the base for the most efficient and productive agricultural enterprise on earth? The farmers of America could feed the world if we had a system for distributing it and someone to pay for it. The results of the United States energy boom are a magnificent tribute to American enterprise and ingenuity, the envy of the world. But now we are in transition. Conflicts in the Middle East endanger our oil supply, and cheap energy is no longer assured. We are confused as we face the necessity of developing a lifestyle that is based on frugality, optimism, and cooperation rather than an economy based on an ever-expanding consumerism.

Christians are called to show the way. A song reminds us, "Tis a gift to be simple." The teachings of Jesus remind us that life does not consist of the abundance of things we possess. Energy-altered lifestyles may lie ahead, but the quality of life need not suffer. It could actually improve, in that it will ultimately be more interesting and less stressful. We should not equate frugality with deprivation. The Latin origin of the word means "useful" or "worthy." The frugal life in the future can be one which retains that which is useful and worthwhile.

The frugal life is everything from wearing a sweater indoors during winter, to turning off unwanted lights, to developing new skills. It means buying or making durable products that can be used and reused, worn and repaired, rather than briefly enjoyed and then discarded. Ask, "Will it meet my need?" rather than, "Does it look good?"

A pastor reported to me that while leading a work project at Red Bird Mission in southern Kentucky, he spent the night in the home of the one of the families. Things were a little spare. As he went to his bedroom, his host said, "Down here we often use the phrase: 'If you want anything we don't have, just ask for it and we will show you how to get along without it.'" More of us can learn that wisdom. If we live in shalom with nature, if we learn to say "enough is enough," we may actually find the quality of life enhanced.

Adjustments in our way of thinking will be required, of course, if we move from an economy based on consumption to one that focuses on conservation. The element of pride will become important. The civil rights movement coined the phrase "black is beautiful." Now we are talking about "small is beautiful." We will soon be looking to the creativity of our own hands. We will develop self-reliance. We will take pride in what we can do for ourselves.

I think a new growth ethic is emerging. The old ethic encouraged rapid material growth powered by technological innovation, supported by exuberant optimism, measured and symbolized by Gross National Product. But a new kind of thinking about growth is now in evidence. Every time the pollsters take our national pulse, they discover a deeper alienation from the idea that more and more is better and better. A majority of Americans say that doing without something and living a more austere life would be a good thing.

A columnist tells of shopping in a store and overhearing a woman say, "I couldn't possibly live without one of those." She was looking at a kitchen appliance. Obviously, she did not intend to be taken seriously. Most of the possessions we enjoy, and are glad to have, we know we could live without. But there are things we *can't* do without. We can live comfortably without elaborate houses and furnishings but not without freedom and love for others. We can live without television and theaters but not without ideas and the capacity to develop them. We can live without luxurious cars and microwave ovens but not without the spiritual energy and motivation to be active. Jesus said, "We do not live by bread alone." There is biblical authority for knowing we will never *have* to do without those things we really *can't* do without. They have their source in God and are therefore available to us in abundance. Referring to the necessities of existence, Jesus said:

> Do not worry about your life, what you will eat or what you will drink, or about your body, what you will wear. Is not life more than food, and the body more than clothing? . . . if God so clothes the grass of the field, which is alive today and tomorrow is thrown into the oven, will he not much more clothe you—you of little faith? . . . your heavenly Father knows that you need all these things (Matt. 6:25-32).

Having this assurance, we can focus our efforts on developing spiritual, emotional, and intellectual resources that make for the genuinely abundant life.

The Shabbat is one of the more important of Old Testament concepts. It is not rest per se, it is rest in the sense of the reestablishment of complete harmony between human beings and between them and nature. Nothing must be destroyed and nothing built. On the Shabbat one lives as if one has nothing, pursuing no aim except being, that is, expressing one's essential powers: praying, studying, eating, drinking, singing, making love. It is a day of joy because it is the day when you are fully yourself. It is a time of shalom.

Stewardship

Steward means keeper, caretaker, custodian. We are keepers, for a short time, of the household called earth. Ecology, incidentally, comes from a Greek word meaning "house" and is concerned with the principles and practices of keeping the household of nature in order.

The earth belongs as much to those who are to come after us as it belongs to us. We have no right to deprive them of benefits it is in our power to bequeath. I read a study of the Amish, those sturdy, independent people who stay close to the soil, driving their horses and buggies. It said that the goal of each generation of Amish families is to leave the soil for the next generation in better condition than they received it.

In the earlier years of our nation, the frontier mentality domi-
nated. It was assumed that there would always be more land, more
space, more timber, more water. Natural resources were viewed as
inexhaustible. And, in a sense they were. Population was small and
there were thousands of miles on out West. Hence the phrase, "Go
west, young man." Unlimited resources and opportunities were
waiting.

A spacecraft economy, however, is different. When the food and
oxygen and water on board are used up, there is no more. This
planet of ours is a small sphere, limited in resources, and if life is to
continue we must be faithful stewards. It is encumbent upon us to
preserve what is here for the next generation and to make sure
everyone in this generation has access to a fair share. William
Faulkner once said that God did not "sign" the masterpiece, creation, because it was left incomplete. God left work for us to do.
There is a growing sensitivity to stewardship which the church can
heighten.

A Cincinnati high school student wrote these words in a letter to
the editor of a local newspaper:

> Don't we all remember the morning when we strolled out the back door
> and filled our lungs with the intoxicating perfume of still-misty gera-
> niums and sweet-flowering dogwood? Looming above us was a cloud-
> less sky so bright and deep and blue that we had to squint just to look at
> it. We watched a dew-drop trickle around the edge of a fragile pink rose
> petal leaving a tiny wet trail behind. Squadrons of sparrows struggled
> with bread crumbs. A cardinal streaked before our eyes and perched on
> a branch so close we could almost touch him. We all remember such a
> morning long ago . . . when nature revealed a bit of her majesty. But
> will my children be able to remember such a morning?

That is a haunting question that encourages us to be responsible
stewards of this beautiful planet. We have an obligation to those
who come after us.

If we are to be faithful stewards, we will learn cooperation more
than rugged individualism, survival of the fittest. Science, technology, trade, transport, and communications in a thousand forms
inexorably mold humanity into a closely knit, interdependent unit.
A nuclear meltdown in Russia affected most of Europe. Our industrial pollution and the emissions from our automobiles create acid
rain for Canada.

The Book of Acts describes the early Christian community. "Now
the whole group of those who believed were of one heart and soul,
and no one claimed private ownership of any possessions, but
everything they owned was held in common" (4:32). Two verses
later it adds, "There was not a needy person among them." That

early Christian community did not succeed in maintaining the posture of "everything in common." But the spirit of cooperation, of making sure the basic needs of everyone are met, is the challenge facing us. The Creator of the universe has provided the resources. As good stewards, we must use them for God's glory and the needs of every person.

During the energy crisis of the Seventies, our president announced that our national goal was to be free from dependence on other nations. Vast quantities of oil and coal do exist in this nation, so fuel-sufficiency is technologically conceivable. But in a larger context, the image of self-sufficiency for our nation is an illusion. Our economy and lifestyle depend on raw materials, products, and services of many nations. We must have markets for our goods. We are inextricably intertwined in an interdependent world in which self-sufficiency is a virtual impossibility, and even if this were not so, it would be morally intolerable for us to sanction the present situation where our nation, with 6 percent of the world's population, uses one-third of the planet's resources and energy.

In short term, we may suppose that our national interest requires self-sufficiency, but any reading of the long-term good of the world community indicates we cannot isolate ourselves from either economic or moral responsibility for the common good of the community of nations. We belong to each other. Our long-range concern must be for universal justice, whereby the world's resources and energy are available as fairly as possible for all humanity. A lesser goal is unworthy of our Christian heritage and of our nation's oft-proclaimed concern for human dignity.

It is a sad commentary on our civilization that war can mobilize human readiness to make sacrifices whereas peace seems to encourage selfishness. But the need to give and to share and the willingness to make sacrifices for others are still found among the members of some professions. We also find the wish to give in the people who volunteer their blood without payment, in situations where people risk their lives to save another person, in the many volunteers who give unstintingly of their energies to make the community a better place in which to live. The frequency and intensity of the desire to share, to give, and to sacrifice should not surprise us. Professor Leakey, in his anthropological studies in Africa, has concluded that, contrary to popular opinion, through the long millennia of our development, cooperation has been more the rule than competition. By instinct we are cooperative, sharing, concerned.

But the need to share is often repressed in our industrial society where competition is stressed. Many believe that we can be motivated only by the expectation of material advantages and rewards, don't believe this. Intrinsically, we are never happier than when sharing, loving, and sacrificing for the common good. A good example of this is the international celebration of Earth Day.

The Book of Judges includes an interesting story about Samson. He was captured by the Philistines. This once proud man was being humiliated as his enemies made sport of him. Samson, now blind, said to the boy who was holding his hand, "Let me feel the pillars on which the house rests." He then grasped the two middle pillars, leaned his weight upon them, and said, "Let me die with the Philistines." Then he pulled with all his might, and the house fell upon all the people who were in it, killing everyone including Samson (16:23-30). This strange story of Samson is a solemn reminder. Here was a man with all the gifts and graces; he was strong, handsome, and a prophet with the smile of God upon him. But he squandered it all in his pursuit of cheap temptations. When he pulled down the temple on his enemies, he also destroyed himself. Perhaps the lesson for us is that the whole world prospers together or falls together.

A new adventure awaits us. We must learn a new lifestyle. We must practice our Christian principles. We can discover that life is better and more promising than ever thought possible. Julian Simon, writing in *The Futurist* (August 1983), concluded with this message:

> I hope you will now agree that the long-run outlook is for a more abundant material life rather than for increased scarcity, in the U.S. and the world as a whole. Of course, such progress does not come about automatically. And my message certainly is not one of complacency. In this I agree with the doomsayers—that our world needs the best efforts of all humanity to improve our lot. I part company with them in that they expect us to come to a bad end despite the efforts we make, whereas I expect a continuation of successful efforts. Their message is self-fulfilling because if you expect inexorable natural limits to stymie your efforts you are likely to feel resigned and give up. But if you recognize the possibility . . . of success, you can tap large reserves of energy and enthusiasm. Energy and enthusiasm, together with the human mind and spirit, constitute our solid hope for the economic future, just as they have been our salvation in ages past. With these forces at work, we will leave a richer, safer, and more beautiful world to our descendants, just as our ancestors improved the world that they bestowed upon us.[3]

2

Family

During the 1988 presidential campaign, there was considerable discussion about traditional family values. Newspapers and magazines raised questions about what is happening to the family. Can it survive the societal changes taking place? All of us are "pro-family." We believe in family values. We want the family to survive as the basic institution in American life. There are, however, many implications in this affirmation.

The Social Principles include the following statement about the family:

> We believe the family to be the basic human community through which persons are nurtured and sustained in mutual love, responsibility, respect, and fidelity. We understand the family as encompassing a wider range of options than that of the two-generational unit of parents and children (the nuclear family), including the extended family, families with adopted children, single parents, stepfamilies, couples without children. We affirm shared responsibility for parenting by men and women and encourage social, economic, and religious efforts to maintain and strengthen relationships within families in order that every member may be assisted toward complete personhood.[4]

The Bible and the Family

There is good reason to doubt the Gospels are as pro-family as we often say. In their accounts, Jesus is unmarried and his twelve disciples are either single or leave their families with considerable frequency in order to follow Jesus. And the story of Jesus staying in the Temple when his parents returned from Jerusalem to Nazareth suggests a startling detachment on the part of Jesus from his family. "Why were you searching for me? Did you not know that I must be in my Father's house?" (Luke 2:49). Later in the Gospels, the adult Jesus proclaims a kingdom that will divide and destroy families. In Matthew 10:35-36 he says: "I have come to set a man against his father, and a daughter against her mother . . . and one's foes will be members of one's own household." To him who wishes to bury his

" Dead in Christ "   *Obedience*

Priority Father before initiating his own discipleship, Jesus demands, "Follow me, and let the dead bury their own dead" (Matt. 8:22). He suggests that a recent marriage is insufficient reason to delay answering the call of the kingdom (Luke 14:20). And echoing his words in the Temple, he said that his true mother, brothers, and sisters are not his biological kin but those who do the will of God (Mark 3:35).

If these words are hard for our "pro-family" generation, it was even more difficult for Jesus' audience, for in his day the family was integrally linked to economic survival. Important as family might be, Jesus said it was to be subordinated to the claims and call of the kingdom. This almost seems to be contrary to the many calls we now hear on behalf of the "traditional family." In the professional ministry, we are saying clergy are not to be "married to their jobs." Family needs are to have a high priority. Workaholics who live only for their jobs, even when the job is doing the work of the church, are frowned on.

Jesus tells his disciples they may lose families but will receive new ones a hundredfold (Mark 10:29-30). We pray to a new Father, one who is in heaven. Husbands, wives, sons, and daughters are brothers and sisters in the church. The New Testament church acted as family. They opened their homes to the Christian community. The central sacrament, the Lord's Supper, symbolized a basic domestic activity. In the biblical description of family, its importance is emphasized but it is clear that from the perspective of both Jesus and the Apostle Paul, there was a higher loyalty and that was to those who shared a common vision of the kingdom of God.

Combining Parenting and a Career

The Social Principles remind us that there are many options when it comes to defining what is a family. My wife followed the traditional role of finding her primary fulfillment in being mother and housewife, and sharing with me in my ministry. We have three daughters (as well as a son). Two daughters are employed outside the home. One has chosen to stay at home and devote her energies to three children as well as support her husband in his ministry as a pastor. Economic matters as well as fulfillment factors are involved in the various decisions. I cite this personal illustration simply to suggest that each family must make its own decision in the light of the particular situation.

The chairperson of the National Committee that prepared the Outstanding Mother Award Honors List in 1980 wrote: "I like to view myself as one of the growing body of involved women who manage both a family and a business responsibility with equal competence. . . . We have the objective of helping to reconcile and interpret the role of Motherhood at home with Motherhood in the professional and commercial world." I affirm what she is doing. In most of our congregations there are many persons who do a great job of combining career and homemaking. But we must also encourage those who wish to make a career out of homemaking. They need the support of church, business, friends, and society at large.

In all of this I have implied that caring for children is primarily a woman's task. There *is* a special bond between a mother and a preschool child. During pregnancy mother and child interact with each other in ways that imprint the child for life. But we are taking another look at the roles people fill. Fathers are becoming more involved in child rearing. And men can certainly take on household tasks previously considered women's work.

Children Are Our Greatest Asset

Jesus brought a new understanding of children by what he said and did as he affirmed their worth. There are two important incidents recorded in the Gospels. On a day when he was very busy, mothers brought children to him that he should touch them. Touching, properly done, indicates warmth, concern, acceptance. We sing the song "He Touched Me." Jesus took the children up into his arms and blessed them. A child feels wanted and secure when loved. Jesus was not too busy!

A second incident came when Jesus was rebuking his disciples for seeking first place; they were power-hungry. He called a child and set him in the midst of those rugged outdoor men. Then he said, "Whoever welcomes one such child in my name welcomes me, and whoever welcomes me welcomes not me but the one who sent me" (Mark 9:37). He was saying that he was so identified with children that when people received them they were receiving him, and when they rejected children, they were rejecting him.

I read in a newspaper story that by mistake a child, two years old, was summoned for jury duty. Someone observed that it was a divinely inspired mistake, for children are the final jury before whom our civilization must be tried. If our priorities were straight, we would take money for our schools off the top of our taxes, and if there were a shortage, let the military make up the difference with bake sales and annual levy votes!

The Social Principles do have something to say to those who are in the parenting business. "Once considered the property of their parents, children are now acknowledged to be full human beings in their own right, but beings to whom adults and society in general have special obligations."[5] These obligations include a quality education and meeting the child's basic physical and emotional needs. But I believe that parents are called to provide much more for their children.

Love and give time to your children. Affirm your children. Let them know they have worth and value and that they are important to you. Never play down their abilities or compare them unfavorably with anyone else. Let them know there are boundaries: There are places they cannot go, things they cannot do, words they cannot say. Don't be afraid to say, "No." Teach them by example. Teach them to be honest, trustworthy, responsible. Never boast in front of a child about how you got away with something, such as driving above speed limits or being undercharged at the store. Do not in any way suggest it is clever to be dishonest.

Help your children form friendships. People beyond the family are important. Help your children be warm, sociable, and caring; otherwise, their lives will be very lonely. Prepare your children spiritually. Expose them to worship, to Christian teaching, to grace at the table, to life-building films, music, art, and literature. Let them know there is a mystery and wonder in life. Help them know that the reverence of the Lord is the beginning of wisdom.

On one occasion I preached a sermon titled, "If I Were to Rear My Children Again." I acknowledged that I might not be any more effective than I was the first time. But one of the points I made was that I would express my love for my wife more. When a child sees a close relationship of love between father and mother, the child's love is enlarged and the best of life's joys and pleasures are pondered. Nothing gives a child so great an inner peace as feeling and seeing parents' love for each other.

I would also do more encouraging. I would try to express appreciation and praise. I reprimanded my children for making mistakes. I sometimes scolded them at the slightest infraction, especially if I were pressured and tense. If I had it to do over, I would work harder at commendation and encouragement. No other thing encourages a child to love life, to seek accomplishment, and to gain confidence more than sincere praise and honest compliments when something is well done.

When serving as a local pastor, I had personal interviews with the youngsters I was planning to confirm. This was always an interesting experience. The youngsters were usually thirteen years of age. I was often impressed by their poise in handling the interview. For many of them this was undoubtedly the first time they had gone to an office and sat down with an adult alone. Frequently, my first question was, "What is the happiest experience you have had this week?" Invariably, it would be the memory of doing something well: "I got an A in math" or "I won a race." Doing something well gives a sense of fulfillment, and all of us need to be commended when it happens.

The children were asked to attend six services of worship and write a report about what they experienced in church and what they especially liked. One youngster wrote on his evaluation form, "I liked sitting with my family." No home is perfect. No one is a perfect parent. But authorities on mental health tell us that children have a common plea: Give us a sense of being wanted and cherished, a sense of uniqueness, and you will have given us that which only parents can give and without which we cannot survive. Children are our greatest assets and the family provides their values and ethics.

Divorce

> Where marriage partners, even after thoughtful consideration and coun-
> sel, are estranged beyond reconciliation, we recognize divorce as regretta-
> ble but recognize the right of divorced persons to remarry. We express our
> deep concern for the care and nurture of the children of divorced and/or
> remarried persons. We encourage that either or both of the divorced
> parents be considered for custody of the minor children of the marriage.
> We encourage an active, accepting, and enabling commitment of the
> church and our society to minister to the members of divorced and
> remarried families.[6]

There was a time when the church was not so accepting of divorce. Until the late Seventies most Annual Conferences required United Methodist clergy to step out of the ministry for at least a year if they experienced a divorce for any reason. Divorce has long been an embarrassment to the church. When permitted, it was often consid- ered a reluctant concession to human sin and frailty. In recent years, however, the church has taken another position. The Social Princi- ples call it "regrettable" but acknowledge the right of divorced persons to remarry. The statement also includes an expression of concern for children.

The Christian Century (April 20, 1977) carried an article by Robert Sinks in which he said:

> Humankind was not made for the laws of marriage, but the laws of
> marriage were fashioned for humankind. Whenever marriage serves to
> crush what is genuinely human, then it must yield to the higher principle
> of the Great Commandment. Granted, there will still be many divorces
> brought about by the flawed decisions of individuals, giving witness to

the continuing ingenuity of human sin, and creating a painful legacy of injury and evil.

    There are occasions, however, when divorce is a responsible act. . . . It is an expression of sin in the sense that the partners have failed to attain the ideal, but it is not an unforgivable act. In such a context divorce may be a creative, positive and affirmative response, ethically justified as that option which best approximates fulfilling the Great Commandment in the midst of limited alternatives.[7]

This statement by a United Methodist pastor may seem to be a rationalization. The Bible, particularly the New Testament, does not offer an easy out. But this pastor does summarize where The United Methodist Church finds itself at the present time.

While serving a church for nineteen years in Cincinnati, I discovered we had many single persons in our community. A significant number of them were divorced. We began ministries for single parents and for those who were experiencing the grief of divorce. I began reading what had been written on the subject, discussing the matter with divorced persons, and talking with people who worked in the Court of Domestic Relations. Out of this research I came to some conclusions. First, contrary to what the headlines sometimes suggest, Americans show no signs of wanting to abandon the family as an institution. Over 90 percent get married. This is all the more astonishing when we remember that marriage is not something imposed by society and religion but is a state freely, consciously, and eagerly sought by men and women. Of greater interest is discovering that 77 percent of married Americans indicated they were either very happy or moderately happy in their marriage and only 5 percent said they were very unhappy.

The family, of course, is changing. There are few homes now where grandparents and grandchildren live under the same roof. Most of the change, however, is an improvement. Marriage partners now choose each other. Their children are usually wanted. In many marriages there is a measure of equality which permits teamwork. The restrictions of previous patterns are gone.

A second discovery I made was that divorced persons, again contrary to the usual assumptions, make better than average marriage prospects. Consider these facts. While our divorce rate is the highest in the Western world, it is less alarming when you remember that only a small fraction of divorces are repeat divorces, that six out of seven of those divorced in recent decades are remarrying and nine-tenths of them stay married. These surprising figures should encourage all who are distressed by the signs of breakdown of the American family. Studies have revealed that in subsequent marriages, divorced persons, especially women, usually make better adjustments than they did in the first marriage. One reason may be that remarriages are made with less stardust in the eye and more realism.

A third conclusion, growing out of many talks with social workers and reading the research currently being done, is that children are not always hurt by divorce as much as they are by staying in an unhappy situation. It has been said that children carry more marriages over rough spots than a nation full of marriage counselors. But I am troubled when a couple decides to stay together for the sake of the children. They should stay together for the sake of their marriage and their own lives. If the marriage continues just for the sake of the children, the parents may be doing more harm than good. Children need parents, or parent substitutes, who not only love them but who love and respect one another. To live in a family where daily conflict and interpersonal tension keep mother and father at each other in conflict or frozen in noncommunication may be more emotionally damaging than living without one parent.

My fourth impression is that stronger divorce laws would not strengthen the institution of marriage. The central element in a wedding ceremony is not the beauty of the setting or even the solemnity of the occasion but the promises exchanged between a man and a woman who have freely decided that they will cast their lives together. It is a covenant and a contract and must be subject to legal regulation. Divorce laws, like all public legislation, keep order in what might otherwise be a chaotic situation. But marriage is strong because people have made a commitment and want to fulfill it, not because a man and a woman are legally bound and can't get out of it.

Fifth, when a marriage has failed and is beyond restoration, the creative use of divorce would involve a settlement based upon insights gained through counseling and pastoral care rather than a contest in court. Usually the two people involved have invested much time and effort in their relationship. Let the separation carry some measure of mutual respect. The matter of guilt and innocence is often of little concern and usually impossible to establish.

My sixth observation, based on more than thirty years of pastoral counseling and a graduate degree in psychology, is that adultery is not the major or the most important cause of divorce. Many orthodox and evangelical religious groups permit divorce, if at all, only for this reason. As one noted biblical scholar points out, however, it often happens that the things which wreck marriages are the things which the law cannot touch. For any number of reasons, a man or a woman may in a moment of passion and failure of control commit adultery. The person may also spend the rest of life in shame and regret. On the other hand, a person may be a model of rectitude in public and yet, by day-to-day sadistic cruelty, selfishness, sarcasm, and criticism, make life a hell for those who are members of the family; and all this may be done with callous deliberateness. The sins which get into the newspapers, the sins whose consequences are most glaringly obvious, may not be, in the sight of God, the most heinous. Without lessening the enormity of any sin, we must remember the good news of redemption and new life. To the woman taken in adultery, Jesus said: "Neither do I condemn thee; go, and sin no more" (John 8:11, KJV). He was not causal about what she had done. He was not implying it was unimportant. Nonetheless, he offered forgiveness and the possibility of a second chance. "Go, and sin no more" was his gentle but firm instruction.

My final observation is that divorce is rarely a solution for personal problems which are spiritual in nature. I have seen many who walked out on their marriage only to find that once the symptomatic pains of the marriage ceased, there was a great vacuum into which other unhappiness and frantic concerns rapidly moved. I have become convinced that persons who have gone through divorce should engage in psychological counseling and spiritual therapy. Through this they will become aware of the factors that led to the failure of their marriage and will then face future relationships with deeper insight and understanding.

In most communities there are Christian organizations for those who have gone through divorce. They have a creed which says that there is a spiritual power greater than ours whose help is essential. Through the years I have watched many relationships begin in romance and end in recrimination because neither partner had a loyalty higher and more controlling than his or her desires. When we cut ourselves off from God, the source of love, the springs of love within our own lives run dry.

3

Sexuality

With the advent of "the pill," American society entered the so-called sexual revolution. The Kinsey reports confirmed what many had suspected. We honored the time-honored guidelines of sexual morality more in theory than in practice. But the advent of AIDS, the disturbing growth in the number of teenage pregnancies, the soaring divorce rate, the pervasive influence of pornography, and the increase in the number of reported cases of incest and rape have made us wonder if the sexual revolution was filled with broken promises. By the time of high school graduation, the average teenager has viewed 15,000 hours of television, including an endless array of scenes depicting or suggesting sexual intercourse. Four out of five of these scenes will involve characters not married to each other.

Our teenager has listened to 10,500 hours of rock music. Much of it is harmless tunes. But there are also songs such as "Sister," a tribute to incest by pop sensation Prince, and Judas Priest's "Eat Me Alive," which describes oral sex forced at gunpoint. Americans will spend about $7 billion a year on pornography and at least half of that will go to organized crime. One and a half million women will be raped each year. If present trends continue, 25 percent of all Americans between 15 and 55 will be infected with some sort of sexually transmitted disease.

Time magazine, in a cover story said, "The Revolution Is Over." Caution and commitment are now the watchwords. The author wrote:

> From cities, suburbs and small town alike, there is growing evidence that the national obsession with sex is subsiding. . . . Many individuals are even rediscovering the traditional values of fidelity, obligation and marriage. . . . Weddings and births are up, divorce is down. . . . Though many values are still being sorted out, most Americans seem stubbornly committed to family, marriage and the traditional idea that sex is tied to affection or justified by it. . . . The whole culture is on a swing back to more traditional expectations. . . . There is a return to the

understanding that the main function of sex is the bodily expression of intimacy.[8]

That is the way *Time* magazine summarized what is happening to the sexual revolution.

But a newspaper reporter, after talking with many laypeople as well as church officials, wrote an article arguing that Christian churches *need* a sexual revolution. Fifty-four young people, members of The United Methodist Church, were interviewed. One said the church didn't care much about sexuality because nobody ever talked about it. Major concerns of these young people included: birth control and pregnancy, diseases, embarrassment, and reluctance of adults to talk with them about their sexuality.

Christians sometimes do avoid discussing how their faith relates to the fact they are sexual beings. But the AIDS crisis makes it clear that churches do not have the luxury of time. A new ethic is desperately needed for the growing number of single persons in our churches. Pornography is a huge and flourishing industry, one that oppresses women and children in particular, and churches have not discovered how to disentangle healthy forms of sexuality from sexual violence. Youth do not feel the church is providing either leadership or support for them in the area of sexuality.

In respone to this need, The United Methodist Church has a rather extensive section on human sexuality in the Social Principles. The statement begins:

> We recognize that sexuality is God's good gift to all persons. We believe persons may be fully human only when that gift is acknowledged and affirmed by themselves, the church, and society. We call all persons to the disciplined, responsible fulfillment of themselves, others, and society in the stewardship of this gift.[9]

God's Good Gift

In the first chapter of Genesis there is a brief, yet magnificent, comment on the meaning of human sexuality: "God created humankind in his image, in the image of God he created them; male and female he created them" (Gen. 1:27). It seems to be saying that our maleness and our femaleness is somehow related to our creation in the image of God. In *Money, Sex, and Power*, Richard J. Foster agrees:

> Our human sexuality, our maleness and femaleness, is not just an accidental arrangement of the human species, not just a convenient way to keep the human race going. No, it is at the center of our true humanity. We exist as male and female in relationship. Our sexualness,

our capacity to love and be loved, is intimately related to our creation in the image of God.

Sex is good in that we express ourselves in creative and pro-creative fashion through it. Sexuality is present in the sexual feelings we have for ourselves and for others. It is expressed, equally, in the pleasure experienced from looking, touching, hugging, or holding. It is present in the desire to reach down and pick up the infant or to reach out and hug an elderly friend. This is making contact in a pleasurable, sensual way quite removed from genital expression but no less personal and important. Picking up a baby can be a meaningful interaction with another person. Some women have said that birth-giving and breast-feeding are wonderfully sensual experiences.

Professor Wilson Yates in an article in *engage/social action* (November 1982) writes that sexuality has four dimensions. *Epithymia* is the inner desire for sexual or sensual pleasure and satisfaction. It is your own personal desire, satisfied in a number of ways. *Erotic* love drives us to seek union with that which can provide fulfillment. It is the passion to find, to experience, to know the other. It is the passion that drives the self toward the other in order to experience and know the other in a meaningful way. *Filial* love is the love of friendship, of companionship. It is love in which a mutual life of giving and receiving is present in an ongoing fashion. *Agape* or self-giving love informs and infuses the other expressions. Agape love releases us from self-centeredness and possessiveness into a relationship that is humanly enriching and creative.

The Bible and Sexuality

The Bible speaks plainly about sex. The Song of Solomon celebrates it. But it is not easy to sum up the Bible's teachings in a way that applies to our condition. First, we have to remember that the sixty-six books cover a thousand years. In the Old Testament, polygamy was accepted because every woman, for economic reasons, had to be attached to a male. By the time of the New Testament, monogamy had become established and the strange custom of levirate, which required a man to have intercourse with his dead brother's wife, had disappeared. The double standard had largely been replaced by a single standard.

Furthermore, the Bible did not try to offer detailed rules as much as provide broad basic truths, leaving the practical implications to be worked out by society in a given period of time. There are contextual and generational implications. When reading the Bible we must constantly ask: What does it mean for our day and time? There are no references to masturbation, petting, contraception, abortion, sterilization, artificial insemination, much less such things as biological and genetic intervention. For the Hebrew, sex was good as long as it was used for procreative purposes, for a man's highest obligation was to have children. The New Testament does not have as many references to sex as the Old Testament because the Hebrew background of social and religious concepts is taken for granted.

Jesus did talk about intention and motive as being important. He reaffirmed the sanctity of marriage as an institution ordained by God. He challenged the idea that everyone had a duty to marry. But nothing in his teaching justified the imposition of celibacy by the church or the implication that celibacy was a higher spiritual state than marriage. Paul does at times suggest this possibility because he had the notion that there was not an extended human future on this earth. The existing world order would come to an early and dramatic end. It did not seem important to him, therefore, to waste time on the regulation of sexual behavior or family life.

Tradition

In Hebrew tradition, sex was a gift of God to be used and celebrated in establishing families and having children. In the early centuries of Christendom, the church departed from this Hebrew way of thinking and became an anti-sexual religion. In no small measure, this was due to the problems of St. Augustine. Prior to his conversion, he had been promiscuous. He could not overcome this inclination for a long period. He saw sex as the source of his own struggle with evil. Also, he and other early Christian thinkers were influenced by the Greek philosophy of dualism which distinguished soul and body as two separate, divisible components of human existence. The soul was the vehicle of good, the body the source of evil. Sexuality was a function of the body and its passions or lusts and was, therefore, evil. Since sexual intercourse was necessary for procreation, it was called the "regrettable necessity."

This attitude prevailed through the centuries. Martin Luther, the Reformer, was more accepting of sex and family than the Roman Catholic Church, but even he said it was not possible to pray while on the marital bed. In the 1920s and 1930s, when I was growing up in conservative, rural Kansas, it was not considered proper for true Christians to practice birth control, as the essential function of sex was to beget children.

In the last thirty years, however, there has been a dramatic shift in theological thinking. Books are being published that call Christians to celebrate their sexuality. Dwight Small has written *Your Marriage Is God's Affair*, described as a fresh and positive approach to understanding and fulfilling sexuality. David Mace, an authority on marriage and the family who taught at one of our seminaries, has published *The Christian Response to the Sexual Revolution*. He reminds his readers that sexual intercourse in marriage can be as immoral and exploitative as it can be outside marriage. But experienced by the Christian husband and wife, it can and should have a truly sacramental character.

A sacrament has been defined as the outward and visible sign of an inward and spiritual grace. Mace suggests this is exactly what sexual union should be for two people living together in Christian love. Then he tells a story out of one of his counseling sessions. He had occasion, as a professional counselor, to ask a wife during an interview about her sexual relationship with her husband. She said they had no problems in that area. Then the wife went on to say that before intercourse her husband always said a prayer. This surprised Mace. He asked her to suggest the nature of the prayer. She smiled and said it was always the same prayer and a very familiar one. As they lay together in bed, in a loving state of anticipation, he simply said, on behalf of them both, "For what we are about to receive, may the Lord make us truly thankful."

Premarital Sex

According to the Social Principles, "Although all persons are sexual beings whether or not they are married, sexual relations are only clearly affirmed in the marriage bond." Yet the statement also says: "Within the context of our understanding of this gift of God, we recognize that God challenges us to find responsible, committed, and loving forms of expression."[10]

In biblical times, it was assumed that people would be married by the time they were in their mid-to-late teens. Today, approximately 40 percent of all persons over eighteen in this country are single. The church affirms sexual intercourse within the marriage bond as something to be celebrated and mutually enjoyed. But what of that approximately one-third who are not married?

I have placed single sexuality under the category of "premarital sex." This reveals my bias. Church leaders have traditionally expected that those who are single will get married and that those who have been married and are now single through divorce or widowhood will simply disappear into the closet until they marry again. The United Methodist General Conference called for "celibacy in singleness, fidelity in marriage," but many are saying a new ethic is needed. This is not to imply that anything goes. It has been suggested that our task is to thread our way between two views; the Old Testament or "thou shalt not" approach exemplified by much of church tradition and the New Testament or "thou shalt" approach evident in much of our current culture.

"Thou shalt not" was based on fear of social disease or pregnancy. These fears are still very much with us. The advent of AIDS has moderated sexual practices, and the number of abortions performed each year would suggest that contraceptives are not being used as society once thought they would be. Still, it is no longer possible to build an ethic for "single sex" on fear alone.

In recent years, there has been a slight shift from the traditional Protestant and Catholic position that there shall be no genital sexual expression outside marriage. Today, some Catholics and most mainline Protestants accept, even if they do not formally approve, "preceremonial" sex between responsible and committed adults. When serving as a local pastor, I discontinued the practice of asking for the groom's address. So many of the couples who came to our church for marriage were already living together, that we simply assumed it. Accepting "preceremonial" sex between responsible and committed persons is moving toward affirming union as primary, while still upholding the importance of procreation.

A Roman Catholic bishop, a colleague of mine in Minnesota, tried to enforce the rule that no couples in his diocese could be married in a Catholic church if they were living together. They must live apart at least three months. But even this was a recognition that they had been living together, and I was aware that the enforcement of this rule was very difficult.

In the *Circuit Rider* (April 1988) author Jon Spong proposed that we revive the old concept of betrothal as a way of affirming and blessing couples who live together in faithfulness outside of marriage. He even proposes a ceremony that would suggest a relationship that is faithful, committed, and public but not legal or necessarily for a lifetime. He likes the word *betrothal* better than "trial marriage." Spong questions whether a society should expect an intelligent generation to suppress their sexual drives from puberty through young adulthood.

The church advocates "celibacy in singleness." *Christianity Today,* a theologically conservative magazine, reports on research done among teenagers in evangelical churches and finds they are following the national trends when it come to sexual activity. In other words, church restrictions no longer control sexual practices. Catholics use birth control and have abortions at about the same rate as the rest of society; evangelical teenagers are about as sexually active as their counterparts. We are now moving more toward talk of responsibility, commitment, and discriminating uses of the godly gift. Continuing in the *Circuit Rider* article, Spong says that when a relationship reaches a certain level of commitment and exclusiveness, then a church might bless that relationship. I doubt if very many clergy or laity in our church are ready at this time to adopt such a procedure. It seems too much of an accommodation to the mood of the time. I still think the church must hold up traditional standards, even as it accepts and understands those who for one reason or another cannot meet them. We do acknowledge that revolutionary thinking is taking place, even in theological circles.

There is, of course, another option. Paul suggests embracing celibacy in order to be free to serve a cause which would be limited if marriage responsibilities were present. Jesus and Paul were not celibate to prove their mastery over the body. That kind of heresy came later in the church (i.e., mind and spirit are good and the body is evil). They were celibate because their singleness enabled them to serve God in a focused way that would otherwise have been impossible. They lived with a "single eye" to the Lord.

For centuries celibacy was considered the main door to sexual salvation, with marriage the option for the multitude. Then, after the Reformation, marriage took over the front door, and single people were sent to the back. But someone asks, "Imagine, if you can, patronizing Jesus as a single person. 'Why haven't you married? I have a cousin you should meet.'" Jesus seems to transcend and transform ordinary expectations. Most of the apostles did their work in tandem with a believing wife; Paul, Barnabas, and Timothy apparently did theirs alone. Nowhere in the New Testament is there any sign of preferring one form of sexual witness over another, except Paul's word to the Corinthians, offered in light of his expectation that time was short. Historians say the early church valued both single and married who worked together for the sake of the Lord. Perhaps this is the witness the contemporary church needs.

Homosexuality

This has become such a complex subject that it deserves a separate chapter, but I shall endeavor to summarize the present position of the church in a few paragraphs. The statement from the Social Principles reads:

> Homosexual persons no less than heterosexual persons are individuals of sacred worth. All persons need the ministry and guidance of the church in their struggles for human fulfillment, as well as the spiritual and emotional care of a fellowship which enables reconciling relationships with God, with others, and with self. Although we do not condone the practice of homosexuality and consider this practice incompatible with Christian teaching, we affirm that God's grace is available to all. We commit ourselves to be in ministry for and with all persons.[11]

The *1988 Book of Discipline* (¶ 402.2) adds this restriction: "Since the practice of homosexuality is incompatible with Christian teaching, self-avowed practicing homosexuals are not to be accepted as candidates, ordained as ministers, or appointed to serve in the United Methodist Church."[12] The *Discipline* also says (¶ 404) that all candidates for the ordained ministry must agree to "exercise responsible self-control by personal habits conducive to bodily health, mental and emotional maturity, fidelity in marriage and celibacy in singleness, social responsibility, and growth in grace and the knowledge and love of God."[13]

No subject in recent years has claimed as much time of the General Conference as homosexuality. Before the 1988 Conference, a survey of the delegates to this top legislative body of the denomination found two-thirds of them identified homosexuality as the most important issue. As with abortion, this is a very controversial subject and few minds are changed by debate. It does seem clear that we do not know whether homosexuality is genetically transmitted, learned behavior, or developmental failure. I will not review the various arguments here. Noted authorities can be cited for each position. Some years ago James B. Nelson, a professor of Christian ethics in Minnesota, suggested that there were four primary theological stances toward homosexuality. The first was a rejecting-punitive position; the second a rejecting-nonpunitive position; the third a conditional acceptance; and the fourth an unconditional acceptance.

Looking at what the church has said, we begin with the fact that we are to assure the civil and legal rights of homosexuals for they are "individuals of sacred worth." Any persecution of or discrimi-

nation against any person at any time because of homosexuality is
not merely un-Christian but is basically sinful. In a statement published by the Reconciling Congregation Program, Joseph C. Weber
writes:

> We must remind ourselves that the church is not simply a fellowship of
> like-minded people. On the contrary, it is a community which is the sign
> of the costly reconciliation brought about by Christ's blood on the Cross.
> The basis of the open fellowship of the church is not some kind of liberal
> tolerance or humanistic acceptance of other persons. The church's fel-
> lowship is founded upon God's reconciliation of the world in Jesus
> Christ, the sovereign initiative of divine mercy.[14]

We are to welcome homosexuals into the fellowship of church,
for all persons need the "ministry and guidance of the church."
There are a number of "reconciling congregations" in our denomination who feel they have a special ministry to and with the
gay community. In these congregations, homosexuals are given
unconditional acceptance. There are other local churches who have
chosen to call themselves "transforming congregations." These
congregations present an alternative to what they consider the
inadequate responses of those who refuse to minister to homosexual persons and those so permissive they would accept homosexual practice as an alternative Christian lifestyle. "Transforming
congregations" affirm both the scriptural witness (as they understand it) to the sinfulness of homosexual practice and the power of
God to transform the lives of all sinners. They endeavor to minister
to the needs of all persons affected by homosexuality, using resources from inside as well as outside the religious community.
And their ultimate objective is to integrate all repentant and re-
deemed persons into full participation in the life of the local
church. Whether a congregation chooses to affirm homosexuality
as an alternate lifestyle or encourage those who are seeking to
change their homosexuality, our churches are called to invite homosexuals as persons of "sacred worth . . . who need the ministry
and guidance of the church."

The General Conference also calls the church to study. One of
the resolutions adopted in 1988 said:

> Whereas, human sexuality is affirmed by The United Methodist Church
> as a good gift from the God of love, but a gift that can contribute both to
> fulfillment and to brokenness among imperfect people; and whereas the
> interpretation of homosexuality has proved to be particularly troubling
> to conscientious Christians of differing opinion; and whereas, important
> biblical, theological, and scientific questions related to homosexuality
> remain in dispute among persons of good will; and whereas the church
> possesses the resources of mind and spirit to resolve such issues reason-

ably and in faithfulness to the gospel it proclaims; Therefore, be it resolved that the General Council on Ministries be directed to conduct a study and report to the 1992 General Conference, using consultants as it deems appropriate, including persons representative of the major existing points of view on homosexuality within the church and persons well-versed in scientific and theological method.[15]

The resolution recognizes the diversity of opinion that exists among theologians and scientists, and asks for study that will guide the church in providing responsible ministries for those who are homosexual in orientation and practice.

I wish to conclude this section with some personal observations. In *Whistling in the Dark*, noted Presbyterian author Frederick Buechner states the position for accepting, unconditionally, the homosexual when he writes:

One of the many ways that we are attracted to each other is sexually . . . we want to give and receive pleasure with our bodies . . . whether it is our own gender or the other that we are chiefly attracted to seems a secondary matter. There is a female element in every male just as there is a male element in every female, and most people if they're honest will acknowledge having been at one time or another attracted to both.

To say that morally, spiritually, humanely, homosexuality is always bad seems as absurd as to say that in the same terms heterosexuality is always good, or the other way round. It is not the object of our sexuality that determines its value but the inner nature of our sexuality.[16]

I have friends who are homosexual. There is a reconciling congregation in the Annual Conference where I served as bishop. I want all legal and civil rights of homosexuals to be honored. I want them to feel welcome in the fellowship of our United Methodist congregations. But I cannot share in Buechner's unconditional affirmation for the following reasons:

1. I do believe our church and our society will lose much if it publicly sanctions the practice of homosexuality as an alternate lifestyle. Many people in this nation are frightened, convinced that changing sexual mores are hurting family life. Even people who think the new tolerance is good are faced with the grave problem present in child rearing and in maintaining for their children values which are necessary to the survival of society even if those values no longer seem absolute. Traditional standards, though changing, are important.

2. The concept of role model is valid. Openly acknowledged and socially sanctioned relationships do have an influence on children, for sexual behavior is learned, regardless of what research

eventually proves about sexual orientation. Children become adults and take their places in society by patterning their behavior after role models. It is inescapable. Sanctioning nontraditional lifestyles will affect the way the young perceive adult society, and it will have an effect on the kind of persons they grow up to be.

3. I know the Bible often expresses itself in the cultural conditions of its day, and we must interpret and apply its concepts and guidelines to our generation, but scripture is clearly against deviant lifestyles. "God so loved the world that he gave his only Son." But this does not mean that everything we do is acceptable. We are to conform to the new life in Christ. In Paul's first letter to the church at Corinth he warns, "Do not be deceived! Fornicators, idolaters, adulterers, male prostitutes, sodomites, thieves, the greedy . . . none of these will inherit the kingdom of God" (6:9-10). We need to be careful about hastily drawing conclusions from this passage. The sins that bar persons from the kingdom of God are acts, not inclinations. Anyone may feel attracted to another person, but it is the act of fornication or adultery that is sin.

There is encouragement in what Paul said to the Corinthians. Right after he catalogued the people who could not expect to attain the kingdom of God, he added, "This is what some of you used to be." However, he continues: "But you were washed, you were sanctified, you were justified in the name of the Lord Jesus Christ and in the Spirit of our God." There is power and life and hope through the Lord Jesus Christ.

AIDS

Recognizing the ominous implications of the AIDS epidemic, the 1988 General Conference adopted an extensive resolution. Here is a part of what was said:

Diseases spring from complex conditions, factors, and choices. It is not helpful to speak of diseases in inflammatory terms like "punishment for sin." The Gospel challenges us to respond with compassion that seeks to enable the physical and spiritual wholeness God intends in the lives of all persons affected by Acquired Immune Deficiency Syndrome. . . . In the spirit of the One who makes all things new, who empowers the people of God for ministries of healing and hope even in the midst of a frightening epidemic, The United Methodist Church and its members are called to respond to the epidemic of Acquired Immune Deficiency Syndrome by engaging in ministry, healing, and social responsibility consistent with the Church's understanding of the Gospel imperatives.[17]

Authorities are now using such words as *crisis*. It is feared that the virus is breaking out of the traditional risk groups. Discrimination and paranoia are to be deplored. But realistic fear can both foster a better intellectual perspective on the issue of AIDS and be a powerful motivator of behavioral change.

One annual conference sponsored an AIDS Awareness Sunday. It was an opportunity for parishioners to grow in understanding of and response to the disastrous results of AIDS. It was also a time for learning about ministries now under way through church and community to serve those suffering from the disease—both the affected person and that person's family, friends, and caretakers. The goal of such an emphasis was that greater understanding of the situation would spur churches and individuals to find new ways to develop ministries of love and compassion and to develop practices and attitudes void of discrimination.

I close this chapter with a few lines from David Mace's book, *The Christian Response to the Sexual Revolution.*

> What is the immediate task that lies before the Church? . . . The first step, as I see it, is for Christians to admit honestly and humbly, to themselves, to one another, and especially to their young people, that they are in confusion about their standards of sexual behavior. . . . In the matter of sex, the Church entered our present era in a deplorably disadvantageous position. . . . What I do assert, however, is that the time has come for the Church to reverse its negative and punitive attitudes toward sex, and to take a much more positive approach. . . . If Christianity persists in presenting itself as an anti-sexual religion, it will not get a hearing in this generation.

I would agree. But no longer being antisexual does not mean we surrender all standards and guidelines. Current society is a confused sexual wilderness. There is a call for the church to offer responsible leading that comes from searching the Bible, studying the best that scientists, psychiatrists, and theologians can provide, and offering helpful guidelines that assist each person to seek and find the abundant life promised by our Lord.

4

Abortion

"America's New Civil War" is the headline introducing an article on abortion in *U.S. News and World Report* (October 3, 1988):

> It is now 15 years since the U.S. Supreme Court ruled that the Constitution protects a woman's right to have an abortion. Fifteen years, and still the war rages. It is a war of words, with one side screaming bloody murder, the other adamantly insisting that abortion is . . . a matter of a woman's right to control her own body. . . . The extremes are at an impasse and the national debate rages relentlessly on. And with good reason. The abortion issue goes straight to the deepest and most painful questions. Where is the line between an individual's right to privacy and society's duty to protect the powerless? . . . At the heart of the matter is a mystery that has been debated for centuries. At what point does a human life, with all the values and perquisites we assign it, really begin? . . . Polling indicates that [Americans] overwhelming support the right to abortion in cases of rape, incest or threat to the mother's health. But those represent a tiny proportion of the 1.6 million abortions that take place each year, ending about one fourth of all pregnancies. About the rest, Americans are not so sure.[18]

One pastor did a survey in his congregation and the responses ranged from "the church should not be in favor of abortion; God holds the key to life and death and has never given us the freedom to make that decision" to "should remain a decision between a woman and her doctor." Without question, abortion is the most emotional issue of politics and morality that confronts the nation. Dr. C. Everett Koop, former Surgeon General, noted that nothing like it had separated our society since the days of slavery. On the one side are the crusaders "for life" who argue on religious and moral grounds that abortion is the murder of an unborn person (the fetus) and thus should be outlawed by constitutional amendment. On the other side are crusaders "for choice" who contend that abortion is a right that women must have if they are ever to be free to control their own bodies, indeed, their own lives. Both sides have mounted massive campaigns to influence the Supreme Court. The abortion debate figured in the 1988 presidential campaign.

The Democratic Platform said that the fundamental rights of reproductive choice should be guaranteed regardless of ability to pay.
The Republican Platform affirmed that the unborn child has a
fundamental individual right to live which cannot be infringed.
The May 1991 Supreme Court decision which ruled that clinics
receiving federal funds cannot disseminate information about
abortion to patients has further intensified the polarization of the
nation over this issue.

The United Methodist position, as adopted at the 1988 General
Conference, states:

> The beginning of life and the ending of life are the God-given bound-
> aries of human existence. While individuals have always had some
> degree of control over when they would die, they now have the awe-
> some power to determine when and even whether new individuals will
> be born. Our belief in the sanctity of unborn human life makes us
> reluctant to approve abortion. But we are equally bound to respect the
> sacredness of the life and well-being of the mother, for whom devastat-
> ing damage may result from an unacceptable pregnancy. In continuity
> with past Christian teaching, we recognize tragic conflicts of life with life
> that may justify abortion, and in such cases support the legal option of
> abortion under proper medical procedures. We cannot affirm abortion as
> an acceptable means of birth control, and we unconditionally reject it as
> a means of gender selection. We call all Christians to a searching and
> prayerful inquiry into the sorts of conditions that may warrant abortion.
> Governmental laws and regulations do not provide all the guidance
> required by the informed Christian conscience. Therefore, a decision
> concerning abortion should be made only after thoughtful and prayerful
> consideration by the parties involved, with medical, pastoral, and other
> appropriate counsel.[19]

This statement, with minor changes, has been the official position of The United Methodist Church since first adopted in 1972
and has been affirmed at each succeeding quadrennial General
Conference.

Scripture and Tradition

Since United Methodists emphasize the importance of using
scripture, tradition, reason, and experience in making decisions
and reaching conclusions, we need to examine their contribution to
this debate. The Bible obviously expresses great concern for the
unborn. Psalm 139, which some have called the "Pregnant
Woman's Psalm," says: "For it was you who formed my inward
parts; you knit me together in my mother's womb. My frame was
not hidden from you, when I was being made in secret, intricately
woven in the depths of the earth" (13, 15). In the first chapter of

Jeremiah there is a hint that there is a divine plan for our lives, even before birth. Verse five says: "Before I formed you in the womb I knew you, and before you were born I consecrated you; I appointed you a prophet to the nations." In Luke there is the implication that the unborn child may receive the spiritual blessing of the Holy Spirit (1:13-15). Zechariah learns he is to be the father of John the Baptist. An angel tells him, "Do not be afraid, Zechariah, for your prayer has been heard. Your wife Elizabeth will bear you a son, and you will name him John. You will have joy and gladness, and many will rejoice at his birth; for he will be great in the sight of the Lord. . . . Even before his birth he will be filled with the Holy Spirit." And, of course, there is the beautiful account of the Incarnation. The angel says to Joseph, "Do not be afraid to take Mary as your wife, for the child conceived in her is from the Holy Spirit" (Matt. 1:20). Furthermore, we have the account in Luke of Mary's visit to the pregnant Elizabeth, Zechariah's wife. "When Elizabeth heard Mary's greeting, the child leaped in her womb. And Elizabeth was filled with the Holy Spirit and exclaimed with a loud cry, 'Blessed are you among women, and blessed is the fruit of your womb'" (1:41-42).

One reason for this great celebration of pregnancy comes from the fact that in the Old Testament a wife's standing was dependent on her ability to bear children. To be a childless wife was the greatest tragedy that could befall a Hebrew woman, and when Rachel cried, "Give me children or I die" she was very near despair. Hebrew teaching about sex can be summarized in two simple statements: It is a gift of God to be used and enjoyed as God directs, and its primary purpose is for procreation. The Hebrew people had a strong sense of destiny, for through them would come the Messiah. He would be born of the seed of Abraham; and since every Hebrew man carried that seed in his loins, it was his duty to propagate, beget sons, pass on the sacred torch. A man's primary response to God's call was to beget children. Little wonder all Jewish men were expected to marry and raise a family and that women rejoiced when pregnant, for now God had taken away their shame—that is, their childlessness. God had opened their womb and they were fulfilling their calling.

Tradition is another of the resources we use in reaching a position. Historically, natural law in Roman Catholic teaching has viewed any meddling with the procreative function of sexuality, including use of contraception, as contrary to the processes of nature and therefore sinful. The problem with both contraception and abortion, however, was not homicide but interference with procreation. In the early church, abortion was acceptable until the time of "quickening" (end of the third month) or the point that "ensoulment" or "animation" was thought to take place.

Charles L. Kammer of St. Olaf College in Minnesota concludes that it is impossible to discover in the teachings of the early church or in the traditions of the church a consensus on the question of abortion which could be described as the Christian position.

Reason and Experience

In the current debate, pro-life arguments tend to speak of the human embryo as an independent legal, medical, and spiritual entity separate from a woman's body with an existence and a right to life of its own. The important thing for advocates of this position, then, is to determine at what point the human embryo becomes a *human* being. Opinions range from the belief that fetal life begins at the moment of conception, or implantation, or viability, or at the moment of birth to the belief that the human person only takes on the quality of "personhood" once it has been loved or socialized into the life of a human community.

Those who sanction abortion focus on the rights and well-being of the mother and of the child *after* it is born. They also usually point out the negative consequences of an unwanted child. But if a person believes a fetus is human, this whole line of reasoning is absolutely irrelevant. Those who think fetuses are people sometimes compare abortion to Hitler's death camps. However, those who believe that fetuses are not human see no basis at all for such a comparison. To some a fetus is tissue, part of a mother's body like her appendix. For those who oppose abortion, this is heresy. They cite what they consider to be the evidence for the humanity of a fetus. Ordinarily they say little or nothing about the effects on the mother or about the quality of life the child will have when it is born.

The United Methodist position is that there is truth in both of the positions described here in somewhat extreme form. We do not hold that the fetus is simply tissue to be lightly discarded. From the moment of conception it has the potential for becoming fully human. The mystery of creation is at work. We do feel a deep moral commitment to protect unborn human life. We do believe there is a brief period at the beginning of pregnancy when the embryo has not achieved viability or "ensoulment," but even then the possibility of human life is present and must be respected; hence our emphasis on the sanctity of unborn human life which makes us reluctant to approve abortion. As indicated earlier,

United Methodists do not approve of abortion for purposes of gender selection or as a means of birth control.

At the same time, United Methodists, while affirming the sanctity of unborn life, also believe there are tragic conflicts of life with life that may justify abortion. Our General Conference has made it clear we do not want a constitutional amendment prohibiting abortion. General Conference uses the word *tragic* and suggests abortion is a step to be taken only after pastoral counseling and prayer.

Jeanne Kirkpatrick, one-time ambassador to the United Nations, explains that her position on abortion goes along with the traditional Protestant position. She says that abortion is always tragic and to be avoided, but it's not necessarily always the worst possible evil. The newspapers carried a story of a severely brain-diseased, seventy-five-pound woman, unable to communicate for over a year, who was raped in a convalescent home. Would the right-to-life advocate be so absolutist as to say this woman should not have access to abortion?

It is difficult to be a prophet when you can see two sides to a question, for you are left squirming in the middle. But Christians who are tryng to be thoughtful are often in this position. Absolutist positions on this issue may make choices easier but not necessarily more moral. There are tragic conflicts of life with life in the real world.

Frederick Buechner, scholar, poet, philosopher, writes in *Whistling in the Dark:*

> Speaking against abortion, someone has said, "No one should be denied access to the great feast of life," to which the rebuttal, obviously enough, is that life isn't much of a feast for the child born to people who don't want it or can't afford it or are one way or another incapable of taking care of it and will one way or another probably end up abusing or abandoning it.
>
> And yet, and yet, who knows what treasure life may hold for even such a child as that may grow up to become? To bear a child even under the best of circumstances, or to abort a child even under the worst—the risks are hair-raising either way and the results incalculable.
>
> How would Jesus himself decide, he who is hailed as Lord of Life and yet who says that it is not the ones who, like an abortionist, can kill the body we should fear but the ones who can kill body and soul together the way only the world into which it is born can kill the unloved, unwanted child (Matt. 10:28)?
>
> There is perhaps no better illustration of the truth that in an imperfect world there are no perfect solutions. All we can do, as Luther said, is sin bravely, which is to say (a) know that neither to have the child nor not to have the child is without the possibility of tragic consequences for everybody yet (b) be brave in knowing also that not even that can put us beyond the forgiving love of God.[20]

The United Methodist Church acknowledges that we live in a fallen world. We are often caught in tragic circumstances. Values do come in conflict. To preserve one, we must sacrifice another. Sometimes we can only act to make the best of a bad situation. A pastor, writing to me about this subject, said of his congregation: "Most would say that abortion upon demand is morally wrong unless the pregnancy is the result of rape or if the mother's life is in danger. I am afraid that while this is what people say is their belief, that if their fifteen-year-old daughter got pregnant, a number of them would approve abortion." That's where the "tragic conflicts of life with life" come into the decision process.

The Sacredness of Life and Well-Being of the Mother

In the late summer of 1988, Mother Teresa made a visit to Canada and in a speech startled her admirers by saying that women having abortions and doctors helping them should all be incarcerated. A medical doctor, responding in a letter published in a Montreal newspaper, argued:

> The rights of women to responsible parenthood, to protection of life, health and autonomy simply do not count in this dogmatic approach. Prevention of overpopulation, starvation, misery and the resulting poisoning of the environment equally do not seem to count. We have here a good example of obsolete religious ideas that are in conflict with individual rights, especially women's rights, and which, on a global scale, hinder rational, sensible, and compassionate solutions to pressing world problems.

Many of those who are pro-choice say their opponents are primarily those who have the most to lose from the empowerment of women, either psychologically, politically, or in terms of authority or financial resources. It is probably true that some women who espouse the pro-life position do so, at least in part, because they have internalized patriarchal values and depend on the sense of identity and worth that comes from having accepted a "woman's place" in society.

Jane Hull Harvey of the General Board of Church and Society has said that The United Methodist Church believes abortion is a moral decision and that women are moral decision-makers. She told the press that the church takes the issue seriously by calling for medically safe birth control and rejecting abortion as a means of birth control and gender selection. She urged the Bush Administration to respect the freedom of conscience of women to make moral decisions concerning their own lives.

With the growth of embryology and fetology and the use of sonograms, we now have more emotional identification with the unborn. I am convinced that the future of the human race depends on the growth of empathy, the ability to identify with others, particularly with the powerless. But the focus of our empathy must be on both the unborn child *and* the woman caught in a tragic web of circumstances. The well-being of the woman is important, as are her rights to privacy and decision making.

A writer for a Dayton, Ohio, newspaper went to the three abortion clinics in the city and interviewed eighteen women. Eleven of the eighteen already had one or two children. Five had had previous abortions. Five were married, but not necessarily happily. A common bond was the firm resolve to end their pregnancy. Neither picketers, nor the second thoughts of family members or boyfriends dissuaded them from their decision. And all eighteen decided against adoption (even though several also had visited a pro-life counseling center) because they said they knew they would not be able to give up a child if they actually delivered it. The other bond was the emotion shared by all—the anxiety, the regret, the grief expressed, each in her own way, at the need to undergo the abortion procedure. We may not always agree with the decision a woman reaches, but as a church we do respect the dignity, worth, and right of women to have control of their own lives. In my opinion, furthermore, the life of the woman is of more value than that of the unborn child.

Gender Selection

The 1988 General Conference spoke in opposition to abortion performed because the fetus is of a sex the parent does not wish, saying: "We unconditionally reject abortion as a means of gender selection." This is a growing problem. An article from the New York Times News Service (published in the fall of 1988) says that although most doctors who do prenatal testing do not advertise their policy on sex selection, national surveys in 1973 and 1988 indicate that the percentage of geneticists willing to do testing for sex selection rose from 1 percent to nearly 20 percent. The reason for this change is not only an increased availability of diagnostic technologies but also a growing disinclination of doctors to be paternalistic, that is, deciding for patients what is best. It is important to note, however, that the overwhelming percentage of doctors are against abortions for the purpose of gender selection.

Constitutional Amendment

We believe "governmental laws and regulations do not provide all the guidance required by the informed Christian conscience." The 1980 General Conference adopted a resolution opposing a constitutional convention. The resolution points out that right-to-life advocates, frustrated by their inability to eliminate all abortions through the normal legislative process, were trying the constitutional convention route. A constitutional amendment declaring the fetus a person from the moment of conception would, in effect, write one particular theological position into the U.S. Constitution. Various faith groups, including The United Methodist Church, do not share that theology.

Abortion is a matter of conscience—a very personal matter. Should those who deeply oppose abortion simply ignore what they believe is the spread of an intolerable evil? No, there is always a place for moral debate in society. Can morality be legislated? Yes, it can and often is, enforcing codes of conduct that society values. Martin Luther King, Jr. once noted that laws could not make persons love each other, but they could keep them from killing each other. But morality cannot, and should not, be legislated where no consensus exists. Our nation allows conflicts of conscience to co-exist within a framework of individual rights. We believe pro-choice advocates, who are willing to leave abortion decisions to individuals, are more in tune with the spirit of a pluralistic society than the pro-life coalition, which seeks to impose by law a morality that is not commonly shared.

In general the Christian faith has been most successful in winning converts in those periods when it has sought to alter society through example rather than force. If, as many anti-abortionists contend, abortion contributes to a disrespect for human life, the way to respond is not through outlawing abortion (which only means that abortion becomes an unsafe practice in clandestine clinics and backrooms) but by working to create a society in which human life is truly respected.

A newspaper headline reads: "Battle lines form as court returns to abortion issues." Some social analysts are convinced that reversal of the U.S. Supreme Court's 1973 decision legalizing abortion would touch off political chaos and social upheaval. Pro-choice advocates are saying they will never accept returning to the time when women had to risk their lives, their health, their families' lives to have an abortion. Some say that making abortions illegal would be like making alcohol illegal during Prohibition in that many just won't obey the law.

Public opinion, always difficult to measure, seems to be on the pro-choice side. Polls indicate that 60 percent of Americans approve of the Supreme Court decision. But there is a distinction to be made. Eighty percent favor abortions in cases of rape and incest or when pregnancy is a threat to a woman's life. But only about 40 percent favor abortions for less compelling reasons. We must remember that behind the rallying cries of the pro-choice group and the picket lines of the pro-life people can be heard the ambivalence and pain of individuals who have confronted the complexities themselves. How greatly we need occasions for people to have dialogue and discussion which are not acrimonious. We need civil discourse instead of civil war. I wish the emotional climate were such that everybody could speak a bit more about honest feelings on the subject and talk and probe together, not merely attack each other. Perhaps that day will come if we pray and work for it.

I have a deep respect for the moral commitment the pro-life movement has to protecting unborn human life. Those who are in this movement sincerely believe that legalized abortions contribute to the breakdown of traditional family values. They believe that abortion is genocide. I must confess, however, that I am disturbed by the pro-life willingness to take a matter of considerable moral uncertainty, and about which there is no consensus, and simply impose an answer on everyone. Perhaps the "kinder, gentler nation" President Bush has called for means we simply find ways of talking together until some measure of moral and political consensus begins to emerge.

Important Social Conditions

As United Methodists, we believe we are called "to a searching and prayerful inquiry into the sorts of conditions that may warrant abortion." We must do something about our sexually stimulating environment. We use sex to sell everything from toothpaste to automobile tires. *USA Today* (January 16, 1989) reported a survey of 677 seventh-, eighth-, and ninth-graders in a mostly white lower-middle class junior high in Indianapolis. Here is one astounding finding. By age thirteen, boys who had never had a sexual experience were in the minority; sexually inexperienced girls were in the minority by age fifteen. There is a need for sex education.

United Methodists believe we must also work so that all persons have a right not only to life but *quality life*. A recent headline said that one-fifth of the children in Ohio (one of the more affluent, industrial states) lives in poverty. All of us love our nation, but we grieve over the fact that millions of those who are born will have their lives destroyed by malnutrition, poor housing, inadequate education, and a lack of meaningful work. If respect for life is the real concern, then the proper Christian response is that of creating a society in which life is truly respected. Our task is that of creating conditions in which an unwanted pregnancy is less likely to be seen as a tragic event. There is much we can do. We can work for improved medical care. Our infant mortality rate is much higher than that of many Western nations. We can work to provide adequate childcare facilities so that a person need not choose between a child and a much-needed income.

Talking only of abortion is starting at the wrong place. The real concern is a society which has so little respect for quality life that unwanted pregnancies are both regular and tragic occurrences. United Methodists want to work for an environment in which life is truly respected and the worth of persons seriously affirmed.

Those of us who are pro-life must make sure we are not just pro-birth. We must not be insensitive to the terror of an impoverished woman who cannot hope to provide proper care for a child. Everyone who is pro-life must also be an advocate for disadvantaged children. Similarly, those of us who are pro-choice must make sure we are not simply pro-*self.* Most abortions are not merely a matter of convenience, as some have said; yet some unknown number are just that—routine ways out of a personal problem that might deserve deeper thought.

Personally, I believe the time has come for us to take a long second look at our abortion policy. We must launch a full-scale effort to improve birth control education, to reform adoption policies (it is estimated that for every traditional baby available, a hundred couples are waiting to adopt it), and above all, to assault the poverty and despair that push too many women toward the abortion clinics. We need alternatives to problem pregnancies other than abortion. This takes compassion, financial and medical resources, and family and societal support. As a denomination we must step outside the political debate and see abortion as a moral, spiritual, and theological concern that involves great human suffering and heartache. Let's not curse the darkness but light a candle of hope by building the kind of society where it is not necessary to legally prohibit abortion because compassion, justice, and wisdom exist in such abundance that much of the need for abortion has been eliminated.

5

Racism

I was born and reared in rural Kansas. My family lived on a farm. Not too far from us was a black family who also were farmers. They had a son about my age. We rode together on the bus, played on the same basketball team, and were casual friends. Our community was rural, provincial, and this was the only black student in our high school. I was not particularly race conscious. After college I went to a northern seminary where there were a number of ethnic students; most of them, however, were from the international community. We lived together in the dorm, and there was an easy, companionable relationship. It was, therefore, something of a shock to go to the South in the mid-Forties and find separate drinking fountains, separate restrooms, and many other visible signs of segregation. I had accepted a teaching position at a junior college. Incensed by these overt signs of racism, I went to the president of the college, who was also from the North, to suggest something should be done. His response was that I should not get involved, that the Southerners knew how to handle the problem. After the school term ended, I moved to Chicago where I had accepted a pastoral appointment.

Not too far from the church I served was a black Methodist congregation. The pastor had graduated from one of the northern seminaries. On "Race Relations Sunday" we frequently exchanged pulpits and choirs. But I found signs of racism in this church. Even though we were both Methodist clergy, he had a different superintendent and bishop than I, and his church was in a different conference. Our denomination in the Forties and Fifties was racially segregated.

In 1961 I moved to Cincinnati. I was quite aware of the civil rights upheaval and, with many others in American society, I was deeply moved by the oratory of Martin Luther King, Jr. and the scenes on television of the struggle for freedom being played out in our national life. I was also confused as to what response I should make when on several occasions the morning service of worship at the church I was serving was interrupted by militant persons representing the "Black Manifesto." By the late Sixties, however, the civil rights issue faded from the television news as increasing attention was given to reporting the conflict in Vietnam. There was a general feeling that the war on racism had been won. The Supreme Court decisions regarding school desegregation and the integration of the military led many to assume we could now give our attention to other concerns. Unfortunately, in the light of current conditions, we must conclude that that early optimism was without substance.

As I read the newspaper, I am forced to realize that our society isn't making rapid progress toward solution of its racial problems. In 1988, a black family with two sons moved into a Dayton, Ohio, suburb; the boys soon became stars on the high school basketball team. Apparently some other athletes were jealous. The black family was harassed and threatened until the family moved from that town. Race continues to be an issue in local, state, and national elections. In Louisiana a leader of the Ku Klux Klan is elected to the legislature, having filed down the edges of his rhetoric to sound like other right-wingers, and goes on to run for governor. The campaign is frightening because it makes racism respectable by clothing it in other issues, such as quotas, rights of the white majority, and elimination of "set asides" for minority businesses.

Martin Luther King, Jr., at the 1963 March on Washington, said that it was his hope that through faith in true Christian beliefs, we as a nation would be able to transform "jangling discords" into "a beautiful symphony of brotherhood." Decades after that statement, blacks have gained a fragile new middle class and a troubled "underclass," while the civil rights movement itself has fallen into a neglect that hurts everyone. Yet, there are signs of revival of interest in the unfinished civil rights revolution.

On a recent anniversary of King's assassination, there were numerous television programs as well as articles in leading magazines documenting the progress that had been made and charting the course that must yet be taken. Business, for one, is taking a new look at minority employment because the labor force of the twenty-first century will be increasingly ethnic. A recent projection suggested that of the next 20 million persons to enter the work force, only 3.5 million will be white males, Indeed, the country is nearing the day when its population will be half minorities. Eliminating racism is not just a task for the few; it is an imperative for everyone if our society is to remain economically viable and be able to compete in the world market.

The Church and Racism

The United Methodist Church has a deep concern about racism, starting with the desire to make the church genuinely inclusive. Recognizing this, the Social Principles say:

> We affirm all persons as equally valuable in the sight of God. . . . Racism is the combination of the power to dominate by one race over other races and a value system which assumes that the dominant race is innately superior to the others. Racism includes both personal and institutional racism. . . . Racism plagues and cripples our growth in Christ . . . therefore, we recognize racism as sin. . . . We commend and encourage the self-awareness of all racial and ethnic minorities and oppressed people which leads them to demand their just and equal rights as members of society. We assert the obligation of society, and groups within the society, to implement compensatory programs that redress long-standing systemic social deprivation of racial and ethnic people. We further assert the right of members of racial and ethnic groups to equal opportunities in employment and promotion; to education and training of the highest quality; to nondiscrimination in voting, in access to public accommodations, and in housing purchase or rental. . . . We support affirmative action as one method of addressing the inequalities and discriminatory practices within our church and society.[21]

In the Book of Resolutions coming from the General Conference, there are a number of resolutions that address racism. One is titled "Elimination of Racism in The United Methodist Church"; another expresses concern about hate groups in the United States; there is also one on "Project Equality."

In September 1987, a Convocation on Racism was held in Louisville, Kentucky. It was called "The Church's Unfinished Agenda." The keynote address was given by Bishop Woodie White, who told a story about a football game. A bitterly cold day, everyone seemed concerned for those seated near them and exchanged food and drinks and told stories even as they were cheering the home team to a victory. Bishop White said it was a joyful day, and he and his teenage daughter had a good time with their new friends at the stadium. On the way home his youngster made a poignant observation: "Dad, isn't it funny how nice white people are when they're not in church?" He said he was momentarily speechless at the realization that racism expresses itself in all areas of life—even in church. Why will people sit together in the classroom and work together in the office, but balk at the prospect of worshiping God together? The bishop concluded, "Racism for the church is an affront to God—a scourge on the Body of Christ, the church, and is fundamentally and unequivocally sin."

The United Methodist Church ethnic minority constituency

numbers about 467,000. The breakdown is as follows: Blacks, 360,000; Hispanics, 39,000; Asians, 39,000; Native Americans, 29,000. These numbers represent about 5 percent of the church's membership in the U.S. and Puerto Rico. We take pride in the fact that there are ethnic people in significant numbers in the denomination. But the harsh truth is that our church is now experiencing a decrease in its ethnic minority constituency, even as the total ethnic population in the country is rising dramatically.

Historically, ethnic people have been attracted to The United Methodist Church because of its history of humanitarianism and support of social justice. Methodism has been called the most American of our nation's denominations for several reasons: a connectionalism that parallels the nation's federal system of states; a noncreedal theology which compares with the Constitution's "freedom of religion" tenet; and a pluralism that mirrors this country's diverse racial and cultural population.

It has been the ethnic presence which has constantly challenged the church to live up to its ideal character. Throughout the years, Methodism has been made distinctive by its pluralism, and it has become increasingly difficult to think of ourselves without our ethnic brothers and sisters.

For this reason, the church made the Ethnic Minority Local Church a priority from 1976 to 1988. The General Conference was saying that we recognize the importance of the ethnic church, we need the leadership our minorities provide, and our future is limited indeed if we do not find a way of reaching the ethnic population in this nation. One way of giving reality to this priority was to allocate special funds for ethnic church development and the recruitment of ethnic clergy. Denominationally, we face a critical shortage of ethnic professional church workers. The church also said that a certain percentage of the staff on boards and agencies should be ethnic and that at least one-fourth of its board members must come from this constituency. The church has made it a denominational objective to be inclusive in the decision-making process. At the national level this has happened. Our minority constituency is well represented. It is at the lower levels of our institutional life that we are not as inclusive as we might wish. And if, as we are prone to say, "It hasn't happened until it happens in the local church," then the bad news is, as Bishop White reminded the Convocation in his address, "Sadly, 11:00 Sunday morning is still the most segregated hour of the week!" Much remains to be done.

I did a consultation with a local church that was in a neighborhood facing racial integration. Some lay members of the church expressed concern that the new neighbors might come to their church. I suggested that was not their problem. Their challenge was to find a way to make their church *attractive* to the newcomers in the neighborhood. Integration does not happen unless it is eagerly and carefully sought. Contrary to what some white congregations think, ethnics are not just waiting for an opportunity to attend their churches. The church that wishes to develop a "rainbow" congregation will need to prepare with great care, develop programs that reach a wide spectrum of interests, and avidly and skillfully seek a response from the ethnic community. When serving as bishop in Minnesota, I found several churches with an ethnic membership of 25 percent or more. There were not many of them, but we did have a few, and it illustrated that it could happen. But those churches had made a studied decision to become fully integrated, had brought the entire congregation into the process so the members in the pew as well as those in leadership had a sense of ownership of what was happening, and then built a solid program of outreach. Integrated churches can emerge, but only if there are creative leaders in both the ethnic and the majority community committed to making it happen.

In other words, unless we are intentional and make comprehensive efforts, we will not become integrated at the level where it really matters—the local church. Honest, and sometimes painful, dialogue is needed. A genuine desire to broaden the racial and ethnic presence is required. There must be excitement about the value of inclusiveness. There must be a willingness to admit that we sin when we think of other persons or groups in terms of racist stereotypes and epithets. We must admit we sin when we participate in systems which differentiate among persons according to color and historic patterns of preference. We must admit sin when we go along with our comfort level of convenience rather than calling into question our practices or trying to change our behavior. But also remember this! When we confess our sin, we have the beginning of hope. We can repent of our sin and move into a new life directed by Christ and guided by the Holy Spirit.

There are, of course, areas where we find hope. On more than one occasion I was privileged to appoint an ethnic pastor to an all-white congregation. Invariably, this was well received. I know that was in Minnesota where the record of racial tension does not have the same history as in some other parts of the nation; but even so, it indicates that we are ready to be the inclusive church.

Furthermore, through the years black citizens have often found the church provided access to power. During the civil rights movement, the black church symbolized the special blend of sacred and

secular that makes organized religion a potent force in black politics. During the 1988 presidential campaign, the emergence of Jesse
Jackson as a major factor was due in large part to the support he
received through the black church. This was no surprise to those
who have followed politics, for black clergymen have been preaching a political gospel for as long as American blacks have had the
vote. The civil rights revolution of the 1960s greatly enhanced the
prestige and political influence of the black church and in 1988 Jesse
Jackson attempted to revive the fervor of those years at the ballot
box. Voting and church attendance are statistically indistinguish-
able within the black community: Black voters attend church and
black churchgoers vote. The church was and still remains the primary organizing headquarters for the black community's participation in politics.

Affirmative Action

Back in the Seventies, Allan Bakke, a thirty-eight-year-old engineer and ex-Marine was denied admission to the University of
California's Davis Medical School. Bakke is white. He charged that
because sixteen nonwhite applicants were admitted with lesser
academic qualifications that his own, he was the victim of reverse
discrimination. He asserted that an admissions policy in which
skin color is the deciding factor, no matter what its purpose, is
unconstitutional.

Racial integration and equal opportunity have long been defined
as a national goal by all branches of our government. The Supreme
Court, the Congress, the President have all endorsed a wide range
of civil rights legislation. Obviously, the church must support this
point of view if we are faithful representatives of One whose
mission was to "preach good news to the poor . . . release to the
captives . . . liberty for the oppressed." We cannot be faithful to
the New Testament without working to eliminate racial discrimination, supporting equal opportunity, and affirming the dignity of
every person regardless of race or sex. Furthermore, it just makes
good common sense to send people to school, to put people to
work, to make useful, productive citizens out of men and women
rather than be forever bedeviled by tragic and unworkable alternatives such as ghettos, welfare, and discrimination. But is reverse
discrimination, or affirmative action as some phrase it, the way to
achieve these goals?

I had a conversation with a well-known news personality, seeking his thoughts on this subject. He is known for his liberal point of
view, but he is against institutionalizing quotas. I reminded him

that laws *can* do certain minimal things. Martin Luther King, Jr. said you couldn't pass a law that would make a person love him but you could pass a law that said it was illegal to kill him. This newsman acknowledged this but went on to say that institutionalizing a quota can be as unfair as past discrimination, this time against another group.

Dr. Glenn C. Loury, a professor of political economy at the John F. Kennedy School of Government at Harvard University, in an article in the *Christian Century* (April 30, 1986) says: "Black Americans confront a great challenge and an enormous opportunity. The black struggle for equality, born in the dark days of slavery and nurtured with the courage and sacrifices of generations who would not silently accept second-class citizenship, now threatens to falter and come to a stop—short of its historic goal." He then attempts to answer the question of "why." He concludes that the great challenge of Black America is to take control of its own future. He suggests that forced busing, and quotas, imply that Black Americans cannot make it on their own. But, he says, "Let a hundred flowers bloom." A spirit of black adventurism could lift the community beyond dependency to self-sufficiency. He continues, "Black America cannot lift itself by its bootstraps into great wealth overnight. But there is a great unexploited potential for change at the level of the black individual and the local black community. In the current environment it is evident that blacks must exploit this dormant opportunity. The self-help approach . . . must be initiated as a matter of necessity, not ideology."[22]

It is, in my judgment, unfair to assume that ethnics can find their place of full participation in our national life without some assistance from the power structure.

When our son was filling out an application for admission to a university, I was surprised to note that he had to designate his ethnic origin. The explanation for the request, as given on the application form, was to enable the university to prove to the federal government their compliance with certain legislation. I presume that the leadership of the university, if they had to make a choice between our youngster and an applicant from a minority group, would have to favor the other. I'm not entirely comfortable with that, but few of us relinquish privilege, power, and status willingly.

I am not for the deliberate use of racial quotas, with a number affixed, but I do believe that the use of race in assuring proper representation is necessary at this juncture in our history. I know this runs counter to the concept that only merit should be the determining factor. In reality, however, merit has never been the only factor considered. In Ivy League schools, the children of alumni are frequently accorded special consideration. Family name, athletic ability, and other factors have always been used in addition to merit. At the time of the Bakke case, the president said he opposed fixed quotas to guarantee minority groups access to schools, but he went on to say he was vigorously in favor of affirmative action for disadvantaged groups.

The Council of Bishops assigned one of its members, Bishop Felton E. May, to spend 15 months in Washington, D.C., in an effort to discover what the church could do to combat the growing menace of the drug problem. On November 4, 1990, May reported on his work to the Council. He indicated that while drugs adversely affect all elements of our society, they are particularly destructive in the black community. May explained that he had concluded that racism is at the root of much of our problem with drugs.

In fact, May wondered aloud if we aren't practicing genocide in our national approach to drugs by permitting drugs to flourish in the black community as a way of destroying the black male population. In the opinion of many, this attitude is symbolized by President Bush's veto, in late 1990, of a bill that would have made it difficult for businesses not to hire minorities. In the fall elections of 1990, many analysts of the senate race in North Carolina speculated about how Jesse Helms won over the former mayor of Charlotte, who is black. Analysts believe Helms was re-elected by appealing to white fears about quotas and affirmative action, which were perceived by some as threatening white jobs. These examples suggest that racism is still real in American life and some form of affirmative action, with all its imperfections, may still be a necessity.

We must be aware that racism is present when we discuss affirmative action and reverse discrimination. I know that many qualified white males cannot secure certain teaching positions because universities, colleges, seminaries are seeking ethnics and/or women. Yet, I am convinced that affirmative action is a good social policy, in part because there is a scriptural imperative. Paul in Philippians 2:3-6 reminds us that Jesus did not look to his own benefit but spent himself for us, and he tells us that as Christians we have a responsibility to look out for other people's welfare before our own. Affirmative action is an appropriate way to do that.

America's initial push for equal opportunity resulted in very little progress because blacks and others had not only been shut out of jobs but had also been denied the necessary education to qualify for jobs. Lyndon Johnson argued that an equal race is not necessarily a fair one. You don't starve somebody for a month, break both his legs, put him at the starting line, and say, "May the best person win." The long history of oppression had left some categories of people unable to compete. Fortunately, the federal government's commitment to affirmative action created a mentality in society that it was valuable to hire minorities. This wider conviction has played an important part in improving the life chances of some women and minorities. Without affirmative action, we would not now have an emerging black middle-class.

Affirmative action in employment cannot do the whole job. It can do little about residential, religious, and educational segregation. It may not always be fair. White males may get the short end of the stick. But some who have been the power structure may have to take second best if overall fairness is to be achieved. Fairness, in biblical terms, means "justice" or "righteousness." And affirmative action may be an appropriate part of a larger program aimed at achieving the godly goal of putting others' welfare before my own.

Education and Racism

The national objective of racial integration and equal opportunity will not be served by changing standards to accomplish racial balance. To soften the requirements, simply on the basis of race, is to say to a person that he or she is not qualified to compete on a basis of equality, and that would be the ultimate insult. In the winter of 1989, there was considerable newspaper discussion as to whether the entrance exams for college athletes should be made more rigorous. Some coaches objected, saying it would deprive ghetto youngsters of the opportunity to achieve an education. But one national columnist wrote that nothing is more misguided and even hazardous than the notion that inadequate and even shabby scholarship can be justified by the requirement of social justice. I suppose you can make a strong argument for both sides of this case. Academic downgrading is the line of least resistance but also the path of greatest danger. Widening the doorway makes it possible for underprivileged students to get started but an even bigger problem is enabling them to go all the way. A university must harmonize its civil and social duties with its traditions of good scholarship.

National interest is not served by sacrificing academic standards. There should be no retreat from excellence. The main losers would be the minority groups from which the favored students came. They would be treated by incompetent doctors, taught by incompetent teachers, served by incompetent lawyers! Furthermore, the students, if inadequately prepared, would not be able to compete in a tough job market. But there are possible directions a concerned society can take.

The provost of one medical school says he does not quarrel with the practice of setting aside a fixed number of places for applicants from minority groups. But the obligation of the university to social justice is not fulfilled by a liberalized policy of admissions. The school must accept responsibility for student performance. Faculty must give extra attention to minority students who need it and seek it. Even with such assistance, some students will not make the grade and then must be asked to leave.

It may be said that it is impossible for higher education to find the necessary resources to provide special facilities for all the students who would like to attend professional schools but who lack adequate educational preparation. Yet, money may be less vital than initiative and imagination, as the University of Alabama demonstrated years ago.

At one time the governor tried to block the admission of blacks to the state university. One way he did this was to raise the admission standards. The response of the university was to send seniors throughout the state to tutor black students who might not otherwise pass those tests. Fifteen years later, more black students were enrolled in the University of Alabama than in Harvard, Yale, Princeton, and Dartmouth combined. One result was a football team, composed of both blacks and whites, that won a national championship. In the final analysis, the most important ingredient in such a program is not money but heart.

Something on the order of a mobilization of conscience may be required if the nation's educational establishments are going to repair accumulated past deficiencies in order to make educational opportunity more than a slogan. Justice does not require that a university education be cheapened through the promiscuous distribution of diplomas. But our educational system can do much more toward helping the disadvantaged meet the standards. Significant differences in test scores must be considered, but lesser differences are often overcome by factors of motivation, character, discipline, and personality.

There is much that gives hope. One-third of all black households have solidly middle-class incomes of $35,000 or more. (Seventy percent of all white households have this much or more.) Blacks in entertainment and sports lead the nation in individual incomes. Seventy-seven percent of the players in the National Basketball Association are black, and sixty percent in the National Football League. Still, only one black head coach walks the sidelines of the National Football League, as of 1990. And a black male in the United States of America has a 1 in 21 chance of being murdered, compared to 1 in 311 for a white male. Four million black Americans are still trapped in festering inner-city ghettos. One-third of all black families remain mired in poverty. The jobless rate for black teenagers is 40 percent. Sixty percent of all black children are born out of wedlock. And as we hear what is happening in Washington, D.C., Chicago, and Detroit we know the American ghetto has become a self-perpetuating nightmare of fatherless children, welfare dependency, crime, gangs, drugs, and despair. Yet many are seizing opportunities that are marginal but still offer some hope. Barbara Reynolds, a columnist in *USA Today* (Feb. 10, 1989) wrote:

> The Corcoran Gallery of Art recently unveiled 75 portraits of black women who changed the USA. They are scientists, share croppers, lawyers, politicians. . . . Actress Cicely Tyson, whose portrait also is in the exhibit, calls black women "miracles in the human race". She says, "Somehow, they are always at the bottom of the ladder, the last rung. And somebody is always trampling on their fingers. Yet, despite the pain, the bruises and the bleeding, they did not let go."[23]

Reynolds concludes: "That message from those who started on the bottom rung should be uplifting to everyone."

Full racial integration, full dignity for all persons, equal opportunity for everyone—that's our goal and the objective to which Christians must be committed. But in the struggle to get there, let's love each other, understand each other, pray for each other, and work together in the name of Jesus who prayed that we might all be one.

In the *Christian Century,* (Feb. 19, 1986), Preston Williams wrote:

> Even now we have not achieved full equality between the White European immigrants, the native Americans, the children of black slaves from Africa and the newer immigrants from Africa, Asia, Latin America and the Caribbean. All these people must struggle if they are to gain the liberty promised. Yet if the land is to be good and the nation is to love unity, we must emphasize Martin Luther King's conviction that only love can truly unite men and women of diverse cultures, religions, races and classes, for we all possess equally the dignity and respect that the God of love and power conferred upon us.[24]

6

Aging

While accurate data are difficult to secure, research indicates that more than 40 percent of the members of The United Methodist Church are fifty-five or older. We do know that the fastest-growing segment of American society is composed of those who are over sixty-five. Recognizing this trend, the 1984 General Conference established a Task Force on Older Adult Ministries. In its report to the 1988 General Conference, the task force said: "The elderly in the United States of America occupy a new frontier in a rapidly changing . . . society—a frontier with its hazards, uncharted ways, unknowns and anxieties, but also with its promises, hopes, visions, and fulfillments."

The Social Principles of the church add this paragraph:

> In a society that places primary emphasis upon youth, those growing old in years are frequently isolated from the mainstream of social existence. We support social policies that integrate the aging into the life of the total community, including sufficient incomes, increased and non-discriminatory employment opportunities, education and service opportunities, and adequate medical care and housing within existing communities.[25]

It is not only appropriate that the church show concern for those who are aging, given the membership demographics of our denomination, it is an imperative. During my years as a bishop, I found that ageism was as real as racism or sexism. It was very difficult to get a local church to receive a new pastor if he/she was over fifty-five. Recently, I received an advertisement for an exercise group. It read, "Come help us explore options for self-affirmation for those in a society where emphasis is on youth. We'll look at the frustrations associated with maturing only in order to get to the joy." I like that. All of us are aging: Let's do it with style so we get to the joy. Here are some suggestions.

First, accept aging as a gift. On one occasion I went to a theater to see Shakespeare's *Twelfth Night*. The action takes place in Macondo, described as a truly happy village "where no one was over thirty years of age and where no one had died." That's so typical of our thinking. If it's paradise, then no one grows older; no one dies. But if we buy into that kind of reasoning, we're doomed to a lot of unhappiness.

I have a clergy friend, now in his late forties, desperately trying to recapture his youth. His hair is gray but long. He has a beard, and wears loud sports jackets and boots. He unbuttons his shirt so the hair on his chest will show. He bought a motorcycle. He divorced his wife. From my perspective, he is silly and pathetic. That is not the way to age with style.

Practice telling your age. It is liberating. In a society that is prejudiced toward the elderly, we sometimes feel the need to conceal our age in order to secure or retain a job. I understand that. But accept your age and enjoy it. The University of Michigan found that of all the groups, persons over sixty have the most positive outlook. The children are grown and have moved away. We have reached whatever we are going to achieve in life. There is opportunity to enjoy some serenity and a sense of accomplishment. The Apostle Paul gives us a worthy example in 1 Corinthians 15:10, "By the grace of God I am what I am." That is a beautiful insight.

Second, believe in your self-worth. I know it is difficult to maintain a sense of self-worth in a society that stresses youthfulness as insistently as ours. Many television programs enjoy cheap humor at the expense of older adults. The constant message seems to be that if you're old you are useless, unneeded, and unattractive. This message, endlessly repeated, does destroy our sense of self-worth. It is, therefore, absolutely essential that we practice attitudes of high self-esteem and high self-worth because the crippling effects of the opposite are immeasurable.

The Bible views old age as a crowning glory. It is a sign of God's blessing. If you are old, you are favored, chosen, special. You have unique gifts to offer. Listen to this roster: Moses was seventy-five when he received his commission to lead Israel out of Egypt; Joshua was "old and stricken in years" when the Lord called him to reclaim the land. Clara Barton, founder of the Red Cross, worked fourteen hours a day at the age of ninety; Tennyson was writing poetry in his eighties; Ronald Reagan was filling the office of president when he was seventy-eight.

Experience is important. I read of a town that lost its electrical power and blacked out. Efforts to repair the system failed until someone remembered the older retired engineer who had worked on the original installation. He was sent for, arrived, examined the equipment, took a tiny mallet from his pocket, and tapped a switch. The crisis was over. Later the town clerk received an itemized bill. Services: $1,000.05. Tapping: 5 cents. Knowing where to tap: $1,000.

Those who are aging have worth, and society needs their contribution. We who are now older adults must believe in our self-worth.

I've heard a story about a woman in her middle forties who was disturbed by an awareness of how fast the years were passing and how old she was becoming. She said to a friend who was considerably older: "I wish I could grow old gracefully, like you." "My dear," the second woman replied, "you don't *grow* old. When you *cease* to grow, you are old." Many apathetic older people have lost their powers and capacities to be alive not because they are old but because they have nothing to do that stimulates their minds and hearts. Obviously, we are not speaking of those who are experiencing deterioration because of illness. But one thing our older population must do is cultivate passions. We need "sustaining enthusiasms." The difference between those who see aging as *succumbing* and those who see it as *becoming* is one of attitude.

The Medical Genetics Department of the New York State Psychiatric Institute, after twenty years of study, reached this conclusion: What older adults lose in speed, they gain in accuracy. Three-fourths actually increased IQ scores as they grew older. But the major conclusion they reached was this: Intellectual performance in old age declines very little until just before death. People in midlife and beyond possess wisdom and discernment, and can develop new interests and expand their horizons. The explosion of interest in adult education confirms this.

Third, respect and cultivate your body. Temperate habits, exercise, proper nutrition, and preventative medicine can safeguard health, make us feel good, slow the aging process, and keep us intellectually agile. Within limits our future is in our own hands. While it is difficult for most young people to realize this, reaching some magical age, such as sixty-five, really doesn't make us different. We still have basic human feelings and needs, both physical and mental.

A fourth and final suggestion on aging is to enjoy your faith. As we grow older, having seen so much, it is easy to become cynical. Be assured of the truth of the hymn writer who wrote, "Living or dying, I am with the Lord." Someone has observed: "When retirement comes, we can step into the confines of a narrowed life, lessened opportunity, lowered interest; or we can step out into a wide-open, unlimited atmosphere of deeper enjoyment and enhanced service. All these latter benefits are there waiting. God shows us the way to claim them."

Never was this contrast better illustrated than in one of the Old Testament incidents. Elijah had just overcome the prophets of Baal atop Mount Carmel. He fled for his life before Queen Jezebel.

Discouragement assailed him and he sought refuge on Mount Horeb. In his feeling of failure and uselessness, he went into the cave. But because he loved and sought to serve God, the power of God at work in him would not permit him to remain useless and unproductive in the cave. The inspiration came: "Go out and stand on the mountain before the Lord" (1 Kings 19:11). In other words, turn your back on limitation. Go forth and meet the world with its problems and opportunities and listen for the still small voice of God.

In a report to the 1988 General Conference, the Task Force on Older Adult Ministries proclaimed:

> We believe that older adults must have the opportunity to reaffirm their faith and commitment to Christ and the Church at this significant period in their lives, to be nurtured in the faith, and to rejoice in the Christian hope. We also believe that it is imperative that older adults have a voice in planning ministries and in forming policies related to their own age group. We join them, and one another, in joy and in sorrow, in life and in death, and face the future with the assurance that God is with us. Thanks be to God!

7

Alcohol

I was ordained an elder in 1947. At that time all persons seeking to be clergy in The Methodist Church were asked if they would abstain from the use of alcohol and tobacco. In 1968, at the time of the merger between the Evangelical United Brethren and Methodist Churches, it was decided that singling out alcohol and tobacco without a reference to other possible addictions was not particularly helpful. The question prospective clergy are now asked in our denomination is:

> For the sake of the mission of Jesus Christ in the world and the most effective witness to the Christian gospel, and in consideration of your influence as an ordained minister, are you willing to make a complete dedication of yourself to the highest ideals of the Christian life; and to this end will you agree to exercise responsible self-control by personal habits conducive to physical health, intentional intellectual development, fidelity in marriage and celibacy in singleness, social responsibility, and growth in grace and the knowledge and love of God?[26]

Obviously, this question is more comprehensive than the earlier one. If a prospective clergyperson in our denomination takes it seriously, as I would hope all do, it would lead to a thoughtful, responsible lifestyle that would be a positive influence. Unfortunately, the removal of the earlier restriction led some to assume that the new United Methodist denomination was indifferent to personal habits. In fact, after the 1968 General Conference, one newspaper carried a headline that said: "Methodist Clergy May Now Smoke and Drink," which was certainly not the intent of the new phrasing.

The United Methodist Church has a long tradition of opposing the manufacture and sale of alcohol. This goes back to the early days of the church when there was a struggle on the frontier for the "soul" of new and emerging communities. Would the dominant influence be the saloon or the church?

Our deep-rooted opposition to the use of alcoholic beverages and the traffic in them goes back, of course, to John Wesley himself. In his original General Rules there were listed as evils to be avoided, "drunkenness, buying or selling spirituous liquors, or drinking them (unless in cases of extreme necessity)." We will not enter in detail into the stages by which American Methodism, from the 1780s onward, wrestled with the problem. Through the years, however, the prevailing attitude was that an ordained minister should forfeit his ministerial standing if convicted of making, selling, or drinking spirituous liquors. For the lay membership Wesley's rule was advisory but not mandatory in the law of the church. By the 1840s the general outlines of the major approaches used by the temperance movement had been initiated. Temperance societies were formed. Signatures to total abstinence pledges were gathered. Political pressure was directed toward preventing the issuance of liquor licenses, and prohibition was envisaged as a not too distant goal. And at least a beginning was made in the recognition that alcoholism is a disease, with the alcoholic someone in need of help and understanding rather than blame.

An important historical footnote is the role of the temperance movement in bringing other reforms to our national life. Frances Willard, long president of the Woman's Christian Temperance Union, which was founded in 1874, broadened the range of that organization to include equal suffrage for women, government regulation of monopolies, direct voting for President, and various other political issues. On the other hand, the Prohibition party, organized in 1869, and the Anti-Saloon League had a very narrow focus, concerned primarily with combatting alcohol.

In the early 1930s Prohibition was repealed, to the great dismay of many Methodists. The prevailing sentiment of the General Conference of the Methodist Episcopal Church North to this event was expressed in the Episcopal address when the bishop said: "Since the closing days of the last General Conference the Eighteenth Amendment has been repealed. . . . We now proclaim to our country and to the world the intent of the Church to continue a relentless fight against the beverage liquor trade. The liquor traffic is inherently immoral. Legalizing it did not change its character."

That statement represents the thinking of the "official church." But what of the laity? A questionnaire taken in the early 1960s found that over 56 percent of Methodists (this was before Union) practiced total abstinence from alcohol. However, 26.5 percent said: "I, as a Christian, may use alcoholic beverages as long as I do so temperately and within reason." The rest of the membership found itself somewhere in between. It is probably safe to assume that today United Methodists would be rather evenly divided in their opinions on this subject. The official position of the church is expressed in the Social Principles in the following statement:

We affirm our long-standing support of abstinence from alcohol as a faithful witness to God's liberating and redeeming love for persons. We also recommend abstinence from the use of marijuana and any illegal drugs. As the use of alcohol is a major factor in both disease and death, we support educational programs encouraging abstinence from such use.

Millions of living human beings are testimony to the beneficial consequences of therapeutic drug use, and millions of others are testimony to the detrimental consequences of drug misuse. We encourage wise policies relating to the availability of potentially beneficial or potentially damaging prescription and over-the-counter drugs; . . . We support regulations that protect society from users of drugs of any kind where it can be shown that a clear and present social danger exists. The drug dependent person is an individual of infinite human worth in need of treatment and rehabilitation, and misuse should be viewed as a symptom of underlying disorders for which remedies should be sought.[27]

Current Alcohol Concerns

We all know that the United States has a drug problem which is snowballing. The dealers are reaching into the homes of all classes. Experimenting with drugs and addiction are found among all ages and backgrounds. But slowly we are beginning to realize our greatest drug problem is not marijuana or crack or heroin. It is alcohol. Because of its social acceptance, alcohol is rarely thought of as a drug. However, based on scientific fact, it is a drug, and it belongs to the category of anesthetics. When abused as other drugs it embodies the same risks of dangerous consequences. *U.S. News and World Report,* in the November 30, 1987, issue, stated that 18 million Americans were problem drinkers and 10 million of them were suffering from alcoholism. Alcohol claims at least 100,000 lives per year, 25 times as many as all illegal drugs combined. Two of every three adults drink, but only 10 percent of them consume half of the liquor. Two of every three high school seniors have drunk alcohol within the last month. By the age of 18, a child will have seen 100,000 beer commercials. The economic costs to society of alcoholism and alcohol abuse are estimated at nearly $117 billion a year—including $18 billion from premature deaths, $66 billion in reduced work effort, $13 billion for treatments. One family in four has been troubled by alcohol, but a new Gallup poll finds only 17 percent of Americans in favor of a return to Prohibition.

Those are the bare statistics. All of us, of course, have our real-life stories that go with the data. We are now learning that alcoholism amounts to more than just odd intervals of strange, and sometimes comic, behavior. For years members of Alcoholics Anonymous have been telling us, with awesome simplicity, that drinking made their lives unmanageable. AlAnon is now bringing the news that relatives of drinkers also suffer. And children of alcoholics bring us new insight into alcoholism's effects on the more than 28 million Americans who have seen at least one parent in the throes of the afliction. Imagine children who live in a chaotic house, ride in a vehicle with a drunk driver, and have no one to talk to about the terror. Children of alcoholics may find it difficult to have intimate relationships because they are afraid to trust or experience joy. They are also prone to marry alcoholics or other severely troubled people because they're willing to accept unacceptable behavior. Many seem to actually be addicted to domestic turmoil. Those who work with alcoholics now recognize that alcoholism is not just an illness that affects bodily organs but a malady that affects families. It has been said that the worst single feature of alcoholism is that it causes people to be unreasonably angry at the people they love most. The 7 million COAs (children of alcoholics) live in a state of constant anxiety because they never know what to expect.

Society Becoming Less Tolerant

In 1989, Kitty Dukakis, wife of Massachusetts Governor Michael Dukakis, entered a facility for treatment for alcohol abuse. She described the weeks before seeking treatment as "terribly lonely and painful." She also said, in a speech following her release, that contemporary society reserves a special stigma for women who become dependent on drugs. Dukakis went public with her battle. As a result, many people were helped. Many benefitted from her attempts to educate the public on such a common problem. Perhaps others were encouraged to seek help after reading that such a well-known public figure sought help for her addiction. Bringing such situations into the public consciousness makes families and society less tolerant of continued abuse. There is a growing conviction that persons with problems must seek help and find a way of controlling, if not curing, their problem.

And in the winter of 1989, America's attention was focused on the Senate debate concerning the confirmation of John Tower as Secretary of Defense. The newspaper accounts of the event said the rejection by the Senate came after six days of often bitter and divisive debate that focused on the former Texas senator's drinking habits, his behavior toward women, and his business dealings with defense contractors. It seems to be general knowledge that alcoholism is an occupational disease among politicians. Washington, DC, has the highest per capita alcohol consumption rate in the country. Until recently, a legislator's drinking was no one's business but his or her own. John Tower's confirmation battle may signal a shift. The extraordinary sight of senators publicly debating their former colleague's drinking habits shows that an official's alcohol use—especially if that person is slated for a sensitive post—is now considered relevant to that person's ability to serve effectively.

With the social and economic costs of excessive alcohol use so high, a new temperance era is emerging. We're not heading to Prohibition again. Having wine with dinner or a beer with the bowling team remains socially acceptable for most people. But the Medical Research Institute of San Francisco has been quoted as saying that drinking is less and less a part of personal and professional lives. The net result is a decline in drinking. Per capita alcohol consumption, which peaked in 1981 at 2.75 gallons, was down to 2.58 gallons by 1986, government studies show. And the social movement against inappropriate drinking, especially drinking and driving, is steadily gaining momentum. Mothers Against Drunk Driving (MADD), formed in 1980, now has 2.8 million members and supporters in almost 400 chapters. Students Against Driving Drunk (SADD), founded in 1981, now has 25,000 chapters and 5 million members in middle schools (7,000), high schools (17,000), and colleges (1,500). While many teens will not say no to alcohol, they will say no to drunk driving. Most of these secular groups are not working toward an alcohol-free society, but toward making intoxication unacceptable because it has proven to be dangerous. The movement for responsible drinking already has won some battles. Alcohol-related highway fatalities are dropping. Many states have passed tough drunk driving laws.

Because of recent legislation, alcohol containers will now carry warnings that pregnant women shouldn't drink and that alcohol impairs both driving and health. But even without labels, the view that alcohol is a dangerous drug has gained considerable public acceptance. In a recent Roper poll, alcohol ranked only behind heroin and cocaine when adults were asked to name substances most damaging to society. Cigarettes and marijuana ranked considerably lower. Much work remains to be done, but the efforts of MADD and SADD along with the public confessions of people in prominent positions as to the destructive effects of excessive drinking are having an impact on American society.

Is Alcoholism a Sin?

The Apostle Paul, writing to the Galatians, says: "The works of the flesh are obvious . . . drunkenness, carousing, and things like these" (5:19-21). For Paul, drunkenness was sin. Methodist preaching in the early part of this century would have identified drinking as sin. Current medical, psychological, and theological opinions differ as to how to describe the abuse of alcohol. Herbert Fingarette, a consultant to the World Health Organization on alcoholism and addiction, has written *Heavy Drinking: The Myth of Alcoholism as a Disease.* He says alcohol abuse is primarily a behavioral disorder rather than a physiological disease. The author is concerned that the disease model removes the problem from the realm of human responsibility and denies the spiritual dimension of alcohol dependency. For this reason, he suggests that the church should strongly oppose the disease model for alcoholism. On the other hand, Stephen Apthorp who is director of Alcohol and Substance Abuse Prevention in Tucson, Arizona, in a *Christian Century* article (November 9, 1988), writes:

> Chemical dependency is a medical illness . . . it is a biochemical, genetic disease with identifiable and progressive symptoms. . . . It is passed from one generation to another . . . it comes in the form of addiction-prone body chemistry and dysfunctional and aberrant behavior patterns . . . it is a primary disease with its own symptomatology; it is not a symptom of some other serious problem. It is a progressive disease in that the physical, spiritual, and emotional symptoms become worse. Chemical dependency is also a fatal disease unless the use is permanently stopped.[28]

J. Keith Miller in *Sin, the Ultimate Deadly Addiction,* indicates that specific sinful acts are not what constitute sin. They are only symptoms of a basic and all-encompassing self-centeredness, an attitude that colors every relationship, including our relationship with God. It is this deeper, more central attitude that leads to all the thoughts and actions we call sins. "Sin, in this view, is about our apparent inability to say no to our need to control people, places, and things in order to implement our self-centered desires." The "blinding self-absorption called Sin," Miller continues, is the same underlying dynamic at work in the life of the chemical addict. "Sin is the universal addiction to self that develops when individuals put themselves in the center of their personal world in a way that leads to abuse of others and self. Sin causes sinners to seek instant gratification, to be first, and to get more than their share—now."

Understood in these terms, I suppose we could say that alcoholism is a sin in that alcoholics put their own needs first. Family, community responsibility, nothing matters as much as satisfying the physical and emotional craving that can only be satiated by the drug of alcohol. But is the desire for alcohol caused by genetics, by "wrong desire," by early environment, or by some other factor? The experts do not seem to be of one mind except to agree that some persons are prone to alcoholism while others are not.

As a church, we have long had an interest in alcohol-related problems. At the same time, we confess some conflict between those who look upon alcohol as a basic evil and the use of it as a fundamental sin against God and those who look upon it as a social problem which calls the committed Christian to seek answers and alternatives while acknowledging its presence and its probable continued existence in our society. In the old stance of the church, it was assumed by some that if a person drank or did not believe in prohibition, that person was simply not a Christian. The result of this, all too frequently, was a rejection by the church of both drinking and the drinker. The image of the church was largely negative, excessively pious, moralistic and judgmental. Even today the abstinence churches tend to ignore the alcoholic, and churches in the moderation tradition tend to ignore the problems of non-addictive social drinking. I do think, however, that there is a new stance emerging which holds hope and excitement for the church and for the individuals toward whom the church's message of love and reconciliation can and will be directed. This stance is characterized by freedom, concern, and responsible activity. In this approach, the individual is considered to be free to establish his or her own style of practicing sobriety but is not abandoned to drink in a way detrimental to the self or to others.

Thomas Shipp, former pastor of Lovers Lane United Methodist Church in Dallas (which for many years carried out an extensive and effective program with alcoholics), observed that many clergy and some parishioners do a better job of pointing the finger than in helping the alcoholic find a way. He has suggested that when the alcoholic appeals to the church for help, the church must be prepared to offer a step-by-step program which assures a future of hope and fulfillment.

How the Church Can Help

As the Social Principles remind us, "We support educational programs." The church must study and become informed. For instance, Frederick Goodwin, head of the Alcohol, Drug Abuse and Mental Health Administration, in an article in *USA Today* (March 9, 1989), refutes some of the myths surrounding dependency. Alcoholism is not just a reaction to stress. There are persons who may use alcohol at times to handle stress but alcoholics are vulnerable, and much of that vulnerability is genetic. I think we can safely assume some persons are more predisposed to alcohol abuse than others. A second myth he refutes is that all alcoholism is the same. He suggests there are at least two distinctive patterns. The most common pattern is when alcoholism creeps up on a person through midlife; in this pattern, a person drinks more and more under stress and gradually slips into dependency. The second type of alcoholism has an early onset and is associated with violence or lack of impulse control. This is the most highly genetic form, passed from one generation to another.

Another myth is that an alcoholic can resume social drinking. This is simply not true. For the overwhelming majority, total life-long abstinence is the only solution. Once an alcoholic, always an alcoholic. And a final myth Goodwin would dispel is that alcoholism is a result of bad choices, weak character, or lack of willpower. The truth is that the alcoholic has a special biological vulnerability to becoming addicted. The paradox is that once a person is in the trap, he or she needs a lot of willpower to beat it. So recovering alcoholics who have avoided drinking might even be thought of as having greater-than-normal character strength.

We must become informed about sources of help. In *Christianity Today* (May 17, 1985), Dr. Anderson Spickard, Jr., director of general internal medicine and professor of medicine at Vanderbilt University Medical Center, wrote an article adapted from his book *Dying for a Drink*. He told how in his early practice he avoided patients with alcohol-related problems. Then in the Seventies he went through a personal spiritual revolution which affected his attitude toward alcoholics. He became eager to help alcoholics. He felt a strong sense of identification with these persons whose lives were out of control. He knew that if the Lord could rescue him from the bondage of pride and arrogance, God could also rescue others from the bondage of alcohol. He shared his testimony, gave them Bible verses and musical recordings, but had to acknowledge that despite his good intentions and genuine concern for his patients' spiritual lives, he never cured a single patient of a drinking problem. He was made aware that willpower is not enough. Then he went to the Hazelden Center, an alcoholism rehabilitation unit in Minnesota. His initial skepticism slowly turned into amazement. He watched skilled counselors lead dozens of alcoholics into honest confrontation with their addiction. Many of the counselors were themselves recovering alcoholics who had been sober for a number of years. The key to their sobriety was a twelve-step program that had been in existence since before World War II; now, in every major city and in most small towns, there were successful, well-run treatment centers or self-help groups for alcoholics. Dr. Spickard goes on to confess that after many years of medical practice, he learned that alcoholism responded to a specific program of treatment, and over a million men, women, and teenagers all over the world were recovering from addiction. Out of his study, research, and observation, he came to these conclusions: 1) No alcoholic should be left alone during the period of physical withdrawal; 2) there is no known cure for alcohol addiction; and 3) instant healings are rare and seldom complete.

In December 1988, *Newsweek* featured a column titled "Hollywood: God Is Nigh," which was written by Benjamin J. Stein. The article discussed how the powerful people in Hollywood were turning away from drug and alcohol abuse and toward Alcoholics Anonymous groups. These people, many of whom are atheistic, are turning toward prayer and confession in the "religious" atmosphere of AA.

Religion, in recent years, has had no place in movies or on primetime TV. But now various groups patterned after the AA model are flourishing. Narcotics Anonymous and Cocaine Anonymous, in addition to AA, all include talk about relying on God or on following a "higher power."

I am not suggesting that the church relinquish its traditional role of helping persons and families in times of crisis and let AA groups do it. We are in the business of redeeming lives. The church is the only caregiving, helping institution that has access to half of all American families each weekend. Gallup polls taken from 1976 to 1983 revealed that Americans rank the clergy highest in terms of honesty and observing ethical standards. This puts the church on the forefront of being able to address the problems of alcohol and drug abuse and puts the clergy in a position to lead the way. But when ministering to addicts and co-dependents, clergy should see themselves as shepherds. Usually, they are not trained to deal with the care and counseling of alcohol and drug addicts. They can be most effective as problem-solving therapists and referral agents. Churches can also set up and promote chemical health education programs. They can invite AA and related groups to use their meeting rooms. In all, the church can help create an environment of hope and redemption. As Stephen Apthorp says, in concluding his article in the *Christian Century,*

> The church should be a community in which people can learn not only to trust in God but to dare to trust one another. The success of the church should be gauged not by the number in attendance, but by the lives redeemed. When we accept our members in their weakness, illness, and dysfunction, and offer them strength and the opportunity for

health and hope, we proclaim our faith in God's redeeming power and establish a basis for faith in each other.[29]

A Commitment to Abstinence

In addition to being a community of help at the time of crisis, the church has a responsibility for education at a more basic level. The General Conference in 1988 recommended a program titled "A Call to Care." This included the institution of a voluntary "Covenant Sunday" for family discussions and local church focus on chemical substance abuse prevention. It was suggested that in a service of worship, families and individuals could be given an opportunity to sign a covenant card to be offered, in private, to God as their covenant concerning chemical substance abuse. A possible format would represent several levels of commitment. It might say,

> Our family, based upon a desire to improve our general mental, physical, and spiritual health, covenants to do the following: To clearly define family expectations and understanding concerning the use of alcohol and other drugs; to make any alcoholic beverage inaccessible to children and youth especially in the home; to have an alcohol free home; not to drive while under the influence of drugs and alcohol; to encourage and support programs of awareness, prevention and treatment relative to alcohol and other drugs in the church and community.[30]

Given our history and our understanding of the church's responsibility to promote a safe and secure society, we must continue working and educating for an environment where children can grow and families flourish free from the ravages of drug and alcohol abuse. We are committed to the achievement of the abundant life for all persons; therefore we have a legitimate concern for all serious human problems, including drinking. We have a historic, biblical right to be concerned about the sick—and alcoholism is related to mental, physical, and social disease. We have a right to be concerned about the poor—and alcoholism is intimately related to much of the poverty in the country. We have a right to be concerned about disillusionment—and when disillusionment runs rife, many persons seek courage by means of drink. We have a right to be concerned about broken homes—and alcoholism is a frequent cause of domestic unhappiness, even catastrophe.

We believe in the stewardship of life and the stewardship of influence. We would be poor interpreters of the Christian life if we permitted ourselves to be maneuvered into a position of silence. In the teachings and life of our Lord, we have a standard for what we believe constitutes the abundant life. That standard means that we shall seek to bring the potential of every person to its maximum.

We live in a society where we are constantly urged to lean on drugs and alcohol to enhance the pleasures of life and diminish the discomfort. As Christians, we are called to use responsible freedom. The human body is a gift, a temple of the Holy Spirit, to be used for the glory of God. Dependence upon that which is artificial is destructive. Chemical and alcohol dependency stands in the way of using our senses, as given by God, for heightened awareness of our world with its wonder and potential. The Bible admonishes us to devote ourselves to Christ only.

For some people, and this is the historic position of United Methodists, the easiest answer is total abstinence. I know there are others, including some clergy, who would say the answer is in responsible usage—moderate and controlled usage of alcohol—to enhance the pleasures of life and diminish the discomfort so that we may more effectively use the body for the glory of God. But all of us who are United Methodists, for Christ's sake, are under the mandate to do responsible thinking, acting, and praying. We believe there is such a thing as the abundant life. Because of that, we are unalterably opposed to whatever cheapens or cripples or destroys human personality, made in the wondrous image of God.

8

Biomedical Ethics

The days of simple doctor-to-patient health care are over. Matters once the province of fate have now become matters of human choice, a development that has profound ethical and legal implications. To some extent, the moral dilemmas we face have always existed, but the progress in medicine over the last twenty-five years has created a sense of turmoil.

In 1969, Leroy Augenstein, chairman of the department of biophysics at Michigan State University and also an adjunct professor at San Francisco Theological Seminary, wrote a book with the intriguing title *Come, Let Us Play God*. In that book he examined such matters as organ transplant and death, reasons for the population explosion, and behavior manipulation. During the ensuing years, our technology has changed so dramatically that he might not recognize the contemporary situation. (Not too long after the publication of his book he was killed in a plane crash.)

For instance, a recent news article told of a young couple who learned that their first child would be born anencephalic—with most of its brain missing. The infant would die almost immediately. The couple might have opted for an abortion, or they could have decided to allow birth and then put the baby "in God's hands." Instead, they elected for the wife to carry the child to full term, then donate its organs for transplant. The problem for the couple is that no hospital has agreed to prolong the infant's life. As one institution's representative remarked, "An anencephalic donor could help give life to four or five people. But there are legal action issues why we don't accept." Such issues always involve religious and ethical questions as well.

The debates are everywhere. On a television program, a dozen of the nation's foremost legal, medical, and theological experts discussed what is appropriate in medical research, especially when it involves human beings. In Holland euthanasia is common although technically illegal. Physicians argue whether placing a baboon's heart in an infant girl is good medicine. *In vitro* fertilization, surrogate motherhood, artificial insemination, prenatal diagnosis

69

and surgery, organ transplants, mechanical life-support systems, and many other advances have made the biblically ordained three score and ten years almost a certainty. Yet it is sometimes difficult to identify these technological achievements as blessings or curses. Today technology can maintain biological life for months and even years after brains have ceased to function. Do we keep the physical body going even after the person we once knew is no longer "there"? In all this debate, the stakes are high. Christians hold individual life to be sacred yet Christian theology teaches that death is not the ultimate enemy and physical life not the ultimate good.

It has been said that most people agree on broad principles of right and wrong. It is only when they apply those principles to their own thought and life that they disagree. This is illustrated in biomedical decision making. As United Methodists we agree that a human being is unique among God's creation. In one sense, of course, all creation is sacred. Land, sky, and seas, and all therein belong to God and are entrusted to us with provision that they will be used only for good purposes. Yet we believe that human beings have a special status, for they are created in the divine image and are specially protected by God's providence.

For this reason we do not accept the antibiblical attitude toward human beings evident in the thinking that an unborn child can be aborted just for the convenience of the mother or for reasons of gender selection. Neither do we accept the aborting of a fetus just because there is a slight handicapping condition. Upholding the sacredness of the human being provides a perspective from which we can at least begin to grapple with the assortment of complex medical decisions facing society.

That said, we also recognize there is no precise agreement among Christians as to how biblical principles are to be applied in specific situations. We acknowledge that on most contemporary medical decisions, the Bible does not provide specific and sharply defined ethical rules. But then a legalistic ethic that would seek absolute conformity to a set of rules might not be very helpful. It is our conviction that God chose to create a people who through a process of moral struggle achieve a certain wisdom empowering them to make ethical decisions. We believe that the Bible teaches that God will give to those who seek and we pray the Holy Spirit will guide us into truth. We also confess that even with the Holy Spirit as a gentle persuader, we will make mistakes. Grace then enters the process.

Even when our mistakes are due to pride or our unwillingness to listen carefully to the voice of God, there is mercy and forgiveness. Though we are fallible, our seemingly inevitable mistakes should not paralyze us. Step by step, God leads us patiently toward maturity. We cannot avoid making decisions. Modern technology demands that we "play God." To live is to decide. Even to thrust all responsibility on others is to decide. We cannot retreat from the awesome responsibility of the decisions modern medicine is forcing upon us. The issues are complex and the principles we draw from scripture can seem to support, on occasion, opposite conclusions. Yet we dare not refuse to make the hard decisions by retreating or refusing to assume moral responsibility for our actions.

Scientific knowledge is doubling every six years. There have been a number of revolutions that have changed society. In the eighteenth and nineteenth centuries, the Industrial Revolution turned medieval society upside down, ending feudalism and creating the modern city. The Atomic Revolution forever altered our understanding of war and peace. Following the Atomic Revolution came the Technological Revolution with developments such as rocket ships, satellites, microwaves, TV, lasers, and computers. These developments have challenged our notions of privacy and community. And now the Biological Revolution is upon us. This began a hundred years ago with such modest but important achievements as the pasteurization of milk and has culminated in innovations such as chemical contraception, artificial insemination, artificial respirators, kidney dialysis, organ transplants, and cloning.

Frank Seydel wrote in the November 1983 issue of *engage/social action* that although the Industrial Revolution, the Atomic Revolution, and the Technological Revolution had great impact on civilization and religious values, the Biological Revolution will exceed the others. He says this revolution brings the potential for altering the mind, life span, and the body.

So extensive are the religious challenges suggested by the Biological Revolution that someone coined the term *bioethics* to describe the phenomenon. Now *bioethics* is a household word. Almost every family faces difficult decisions. When do you "pull the plug"? How far should a childless couple go in effort to have children? Are they ethically and morally entitled to "rent a womb," as one newspaper described it? If only one organ is available for a transplant, who gets it?

The United Methodist Church, through its General Conference, has endeavored to respond to this "revolution" with some resolutions and guidelines. We shall briefly examine four of them.

Genetic Manipulation

This is perhaps the most basic of all the issues and the one with the most far-reaching implications. The 1988 Social Principles carry this statement:

> The responsibility of humankind for the whole creation challenges us to deal carefully with the possibilities of genetic research and gene-technology. We welcome the development and application of gene-technological methods for battling hunger through new sorts of plants and improved crops as well as for healing diseases by new, more effective, and cheaper medicine. . . . Changes of human chromosomes are justified only for therapeutic reasons, and only if they do not include experiments which produce waste embryos or changes in germ cells.[31]

This statement expresses concern about genetic engineering unless it is restricted to research on bacteria that would improve plants and crops and not take place on human beings. That is, programs of positive eugenics are dubious and dangerous, even though the effort to eliminate genetic diseases is laudable. Yet knowing the genetic source of many diseases, as well as people's genetically influenced susceptibility to disease, is quickly becoming indispensable in many fields of medicine. And while we encourage research that will create new plants and improved crops, there are serious questions about this kind of experimentation.

If commercial seed companies, chemical companies, and petroleum corporations do all the research, who will defend the objectives of farmers and consumers? Will food be more or less nutritious, better or worse tasting? Will breeding for short-term profits allow time to take the careful steps to avert genetic vulnerability? Agriculture begins in the seed. The genetic information programmed into the seed determines the plant that emerges and the human practices that can bring the plant to maturity. The future of agriculture will be shaped by the survival or erosion of the genetic information carried with the seed, by its manipulation at the hands of plant breeders, and by its transfer to farmers via the seed marketing industry. At stake is the question of who will benefit and who will suffer.

When it comes to genetic engineering as it relates to persons, we are greatly concerned that we proceed with extreme caution. We know there is promise. Cancer, viral disease, and even certain aspects of the aging process may be conquered through genetic engineering. Yet there are many unknowns in this kind of research. The DNA contained in every human cell is compacted and coiled in twenty-three pairs of tight bundles called chromosomes.

In every molecule of DNA there is the blueprint for eyes, brain, liver, heart, and bones. Directly altering an organism by changing its genetic code requires that the gene (or set of instructions) along the DNA coil be modified and that this same set of instructions be changed in every cell of the organism.

Genetic researchers who first contemplated the problem of directly altering the coding sequence of DNA were faced with problems that were simultaneously simple and complex. The simple part was the exchange of molecules in the DNA to bring about the desired modifications. The complex part is to locate the right gene and to alter only that part of the code. Although the basic idea was simple, researchers would be working at the molecular level, beyond the range of any microscope.

This process raises many questions. As a church we endorse attempts to control genetic disease: prenatal and postnatal screening, counseling prospective parents who are at risk of producing a genetically defective child, repairing or replacing defective genes and their products. But we do raise cautions about possible abuses: coercive, mandatory screenings; discrimination against those identified as "defective"; coercion of some people not to reproduce; abortion of fetuses considered less than "normal." In *Christianity Today* (February 7, 1986), DNA codiscoverer Sir Francis Crick said that no newborn should be considered human until it passes tests about its genetic endowment. He added that if the infant doesn't pass the tests, then it forfeits its right to live. We would consider this kind of thinking as a contradiction of traditional biblical and moral teaching.

June 8, 1982, sixty religious leaders from across the nation issued a statement of concern that engineering specific genetic traits into the human germline not be attempted. I believe this sums up where The United Methodist Church finds itself at this time in our history on the topic of genetic-engineering or manipulation.

Reproduction Technology

Technology in the area of reproductive biology has made great strides, and with each major accomplishment, public opinion becomes more divergent. In 1978, Louise Brown was conceived in a glass dish and successfully carried to birth. *In vitro* (in glass) fertilization focused attention on the fact that technology which was developed primarily for animal husbandry was now being applied to human reproduction. Some saw it as a blessing and others viewed it as a curse. But this baby represented the fruition of more than a decade of intensive effort to invent a way for women who normally could not conceive to have children. The doctor, a gynecologist, fought medical and religious opposition and faced countless setbacks. He was criticized for playing God. After the birth, he was accused of cashing in on newspaper sensationalizing of the rare medical accomplishment.

When this British family—Lesley Brown, her husband John, a 38-year-old truck driver, and their baby—was splashed across the front page of every newspaper around the world, a gathering storm of religious protest culminated in a denunciation by the Pope. But Lesley Brown believes that God wouldn't have allowed the miracle of modern science to happen to her had God not wanted her to have a baby.

Not everyone was as optimistic. Some see the birth as a step into a future that no one could control.

United Methodist ethicists disagreed with one another in their response to the event. One, a medical ethicist teaching at Princeton University, declared that the use of such procedures is morally wrong because it is experimentation on possible future human beings. But another, a dean of a theological seminary, said that the development was significant in advancing the possibility for previously childless couples to now experience the joys and responsibilities of parenthood. He said he could see no reason why science should not proceed with this kind of opportunity.

The Pope, in a press release, extended cordial best wishes to Louise and added that he had no right to condemn the parents. Yet he expressed concern about medicine replacing the marriage act. In 1987 the Vatican affirmed its traditional position when it expressed opposition to such practices as *in vitro* fertilization, artificial insemination by donor, surrogate motherhood, embryo freezing, and artificial insemination by the husband when semen is collected through masturbation.

What is our response as United Methodists? The General Conference has not offered specific resolutions on this subject, but there are some general conclusions offered by our ethicists and theologians.

First, persons of faith must not take a defensive posture. The church has never completely recovered from the fact that when the Copernican revolution came, it was on the wrong side. There is an old saying which reminds us that men who become wedded to the spirit of the times are likely to find themselves widowers in the next generation. But no one is so naive as to claim that there are no moral and ethical questions raised by these new reproductive technologies.

Second, not everything possible is always permissible. There are limits. We must follow truth. We have intellect, an inquisitive mind, and the desire to know. But we must also hope and pray that we have the wisdom to use our discoveries with restraint. The ascent of the human race is always a little tentative.

Neil Armstrong had no such doubt; he was certain that when he put his foot down on the moon it was a giant step forward for humankind. At the same time, there are proponents of "Murphy's Law" who are certain that if anything can go wrong, it will. These two orientations stem not necessarily from different data but from a difference in a fundamental point of view. What we are up against, finally, is whether one thinks that the universe is essentially friendly or hostile. I believe that since God created the universe, ordained it, and orders it, it is friendly, and we can pursue knowledge confident in the long march of history. But as we pursue knowledge, we are still under the constraint to exercise our highest moral and ethical judgment in using our newly acquired knowledge and information.

A newspaper article carried the headline "Womb Service" and told the story of a woman who had functioned as a surrogate mother. The sperm and the egg were both from the parents. The surrogate mother simply bore the child. Her "womb was for hire." In 1988 there was a celebrated case known as "Baby M." In that case, it was the father's sperm but the surrogate mother's egg. After the birth, the natural mother began to demand her rights and a long legal battle ensued. Three things, says the Bible, are never satisfied—the barren womb, the earth ever-thirsty for water, and the fire which never says "enough." We understand why couples who are infertile pursue having a baby with a relentless, almost frantic fervor. But until we have some new understanding, we must oppose any reproductive process that introduces third-party genetic material in that it violates the sanctity of the marriage contract. Furthermore, as the "Baby M" case has illustrated, we do not know what the moral and legal rights and obligations are of the contributor of the seed or the egg. We certainly have little research as to the emotional ramifications for the couple when only one partner is the biological parent. And while the woman who provided "womb service" was not a biological parent, is it possible to go through the pregnancy and birthing without developing some strong emotional bonding? With so many unanswered questions, I must oppose the concept of the surrogate mother, whatever form it takes.

Incidentally, some Jewish theologians have opposed surrogacy on the grounds that because giving birth puts a woman's life in danger, she should not take the risk of childbirth unless she will enjoy the benefit of keeping the child. And some ethicists object to reproductive technology on the grounds that it is immoral to spend time and resources on extraordinary means of promoting births when attention should be devoted to preventing unwanted births and improving the health of all infants. Finally, some persons claim that reproductive technology will promote a perception of children as products rather than as human beings to be cherished in their own right.

It is for this reason, as well as others, that we have serious questions about such practices as *in vitro* fertilization, artificial insemination by donor, and embryo freezing. Treatments which involve the creation of human embryo outside the womb or the removal of an embryo from the womb, raise questions about the moral status of the embryo and its rights. Can it be destroyed or experimented on? Who will look out for its interests? While not all religious leaders would rule out experimental use of embryos, most believe that human genetic material should be used only under limited conditions. Some view discarding unused embryos as abortion. Answers are not easy. Most religious commentators agree that the best response is to see that reproductive technology is regulated, not banned entirely. As someone has phrased it: "The river that is the knowledge of life has been crossed, and we cannot go back again."

Organ Transplants

A 1985 Gallup poll indicated tht 70 percent of those surveyed said they would be willing to donate body organs of deceased relatives for transplantation but only about 25 percent said they planned to do it themselves. This is an interesting discrepancy. Almost everyone endorses the surgical procedure but at a deeper level many seem reluctant to become involved as potential donors themselves. Behind this hesitancy there quite probably lurks a fear of death. We may also find distasteful the idea that surgeons could cut away at our most personal possession, our body. As a result, there is a tragic shortage of organ donors.

A number of denominations have adopted official positions in support of this practice. For instance, in 1986 the bishops and executives of various churches in Southwest Pennsylvania affirmed that they believe organ donation and transplantation are consistent with the truths of creation and redemption. Therefore, they encourage Christians to support and to participate in organ donation and transplantation.

This statement allows for the sensibilities of those denominations, such as some within Eastern Orthodoxy, that have theological reservations about the practice. For some churches, the belief that a complete body is needed for resurrection and the afterlife creates an obvious problem. There are Christians who insist that persons, whatever else they are, are a complement of soul and body, to be resurrected as a whole. "What is sown in the earth as a perishable thing is raised imperishable" (1 Cor. 15:42, NEB). For some there may be a conviction that the heart in particular, as a person's symbolic core, ought not to be transplanted. But for most churches, including the United Methodist, such doctrinal concerns are not a major obstacle to organ transplant.

Newspapers and television have made us quite aware that organ transplant has the potential to extend life for the recipient. In other situations, such as a cornea transplant, it improves the quality of life. Also, on occasion it can be a way of bringing some good out of a tragedy. Former U.S. Surgeon General C. Everett Koop commented that upon losing a child, a parent wants to wring every possible good out of the experience. He and his wife lost a son before transplantation was common. Koop said that if his son's death could have been the occasion for five or six other people to be helped, he would have felt much better about his death than he did. Furthermore, organ donation is one way we can give of ourselves for another. It is not, of course, a heroic act except in situations such as when a family member gives a kidney to another. For the vast majority, having a donor card is a painless enterprise whose purpose would be carried out only after they have died.

Among the marvelous accomplishments of modern technology, the transfer of body organs from one person to another is one of the greatest. The tragedy of one person's death can become the occasion for another's continued life. It fulfills the scriptural mandate that we ought to lay down our lives for one another (1 John 3:16). The supply of organs is short. It is estimated that the families of 15,000 patients are desperately awaiting the phone call that a heart, a liver, or a lung is available. A third of the heart patients and many of the others will die waiting. More than enough people die in accidents with organs intact to meet the demand for life-saving transplants, but only about 20 percent carry donor cards. Thanks to medical research and organ transplants, thousands of healthy men, women, and children are living proof today of these miracles of modern medicine. But more persons must sign the donor cards.

There are, of course, dimensions of this that raise difficult ethical questions. In the opening paragraph of this chapter, I made reference to a child with a portion of its brain missing. Is it ethical to keep the child alive so its organs can be donated? The large majority of physicians and medical ethicists firmly—and rightly— oppose prematurely ending the anencephalic's life in order to use its organs. But should the child, even though brain dead, be put on a respirator merely to keep the organs viable and useful in a transplant? Or is this exploiting an unfortunate, helpless human being?

There are two biblical insights that might help us make a decision. First, the Bible does call us to care for the weak and the helpless and no one is more weak and helpless than an anencephalic. But we are also called to promote life, not merely guard it. Jesus said he had come to give the abundant life. If some babies will live a richer, longer life after receiving organs from anencephalics, this might encourage us to think long and hard about prolonging the baby's life to do such transplants. Still we proceed with caution. Should we regard anencephalic babies (about 2,500 are born every year) as a new and welcome source of organs? Or should we regard their use as a dangerous precedent, a crack in the door that will allow us to use others who are not exactly, not legally, dead?

The director of the Center for Biomedical Ethics at the University of Minnesota says it is highly desirable to make it possible for these infants to be used as donors since there are thousands of children who die each year for want of a donor. He points out that the diagnosis of anencephalia is clearcut and reliable. There is no danger of confusing these babies with babies with birth defects who might have some hope of mental life. But a professor of medical ethics at the same university objects because of a fear that such technology takes emphasis away from the medical protection of human life.

Where are we as United Methodists? We are of varying opinions. As a general principle, we come down on the side of life. But we do not want to start down the slippery slope that finally leads to the exploitation of the weak and helpless. Life, even impaired life, is precious and a gift from God. The handicapped also bear the divine image. Treating dying anencephalic newborns in intensive-care units with respirators solely for the purpose of harvesting their organs is unjustified. Although there is much disagreement in our society about whether fetuses are "persons," we have always held that a live-born infant, regardless of the degree of retardation, is a person with both legal and moral rights. Therefore, no measures should be taken to hasten the death of the anencephalic, and no organ procurement should proceed until brain death is certified according to normal medical procedures.

Euthanasia

The 1988 General Conference in a resolution on aging said: "Life in the later years has caused older persons to ask two questions: How can my life be maintained? What gives meaning and purpose to my life in these years? Both questions have religious implications."[32]

The graying of America implies also the graying of The United Methodist Church. Life expectancy is increasing rapidly. Technology makes it possible to keep some persons alive almost indefinitely. How much technology is enough? Who decides who gets treated and when treatment is terminated? All of us are aware of the Right-to-Life movement. Not as well known are organizations with names such as Right-to-Die, the Hemlock Society, and others. They speak of helping people have a "good death." Just as technology has posed many questions for society as to when and who shall be born, in a similar fashion, technology is raising issues about when and how to die.

While I was visiting an 85-year-old retired pastor who was a patient in the hospital, he suffered a relapse. Because he was attached to monitoring devices, medical staff were immediately alerted to his changed condition. Within a few moments there were seven or eight people in the room with a variety of technological resources. Within a half-hour, he was breathing somewhat normally and his heart was beating, having stopped during the time of his crisis. A few days later he was transferred to a nursing home where he lived another six months. During that time he was in extreme discomfort, and the bills exhausted most of his family's financial resources.

Every pastor has witnessed a similar experience. Most families have had at least one elderly relative whose life was prolonged through modern medical techniques. Is there a "time to be born and a time to die"? When do you pull the plug? Did the hospital personnel have any choice about using heroic measures to keep the retired pastor alive?

Scarcely a week goes by without a press report of either an ill elderly person asking to be taken off life-support systems, or the family, friends, or physician of a terminally ill patient becoming involved in a "mercy killing." Some years ago a California appellate court ruled that a patient did have a constitutional right to be disconnected from life-support systems. Many religious and medical groups are against measures allowing a patient, essentially, to request death.

But how shall the elderly die? That "how" includes both physical control over death and its circumstances, and mental and emotional preparation for dying. The situation has become so pressing largely because medical science seems to be focusing its energy on prolonging life, regardless of its quality. A recent conference on the ethical issues surrounding dying heard one prominent theologian say that longer life spans and new medical techniques require new forms of education. The church, this speaker said, must reopen the question of suicide and consider whether it is valid to give back to God a life which has been given. But other ethicists say that to choose to assist the dying process actively is to throw the gift of life back in the face of the giver. On the other hand, Betty Rollin, a national television news correspondent, wrote a best-seller about how she actually assisted in her mother's suicide. *Last Wish* is a compelling, matter-of-fact description of Rollin's aging mother being ravaged by uterine cancer. In extreme pain, she wanted to kill herself. But because she was too weak to leave her bed, the mother convinced Rollin to assist her in her death wish by finding out how she could kill herself with pills.

Assisted suicide is illegal in the United States, so Rollin telephoned a physician in Holland, where euthanasia is permitted. Obtaining the name of a drug and the necessary dosage, she and her mother carried out the plan. As her mother drifted into a medicated death, Rollin quotes her as saying, "Remember, I am the most happy woman. And this is my wish."

Patients traditionally have the legal right to control their own medical treatment, including the right to refuse care. On the other hand, all states retain laws against helping people kill themselves. The two potentially conflicting rules of law are reconciled by barring doctors from assisting patients to commit suicide, such as by supplying poison, but by allowing patients to refuse medical treatment necessary to keep them alive.

The church supports this position. It seems contrary to our understanding of the sanctity of life to assist in suicide. The issue is not, however, a simple one. Some years ago the prominent theologian and former president of Union Theological Seminary, Henry Pitney Van Dusen, attempted a mutual suicide along with his wife as a release from the terminal illness both of them were experiencing. In a letter left for their family, they said they hoped for understanding although they knew some would disapprove and be disillusioned. Alluding to their principal justification—faltering health and growing dependency—the letter added that they were becoming weaker and more unwell. They asked: Who would want to die in a nursing home? While we canot affirm their decision, we do acknowledge the difficult, painful, and ubiquitous issues of modern medicine's impact on life-and-death decisions.

How much treatment is too much? At the forefront of change are "living wills" in which healthy people can authorize physicians not to use life-sustaining treatment if they become terminally ill and cannot participate in treatment decisions. A majority of the states have now authorized "living wills." There are problems with them, but they are important if a patient is to retain some measure of control. The New Jersey Supreme Court ruled some years ago that where there is clear indication that an incompetent patient would have refused treatment, incuding tube feeding, then a family member or guardian can make the same decision on the patient's behalf. However, if there is no indication of the patient's wish, then treatment should continue unless it is inhumanly painful. The court also ruled that treatment must never be withdrawn from a patient who previously expressed a wish that it continue.

Such treatment decisions will increasingly confront society and, consequently, the church. As former Surgeon General Koop notes, "For every Baby Doe born today, there will be 15,000 Granny Does by the end of the 1990s." What is now called for is compassionate guidance for both the infirm and the people making life-and-death decisions.

Before "pulling the plug" there are some considerations that we must remember as Christians. Primary among these is our Judeo-Christian belief in the sanctity of human life, created as it is in God's image. In this understanding, an individual does not have the absolute right and final jurisdiction over his or her own bodily life, much less the lives of others. Our lives belong not to us, but to God. Furthermore, within the bounds of life, what is "hopeless"? Do we not know of instances when through the grace of God, "hopeless" persons were healed? In addition to this, we have not finally solved the difficult problem of defining "death." We do not support the artificial preservation of "life" in a person who is "dead." But only when we are confident that a person is medically dead can society be justified in saying "pull the plug," unless it is the clear wish of the patient that heroic measures no longer be used.

In closing, I wish to add a few reflections on the Christian approach to death. First, express honest emotions. Christians who may feel ashamed of their anguish about death do well to remember Jesus at the grave of Lazarus. He wept. The only complete human being who ever lived felt pain and loss at the death of his friend.

Second, a Christian understanding of death would suggest that when death comes, we shift the focus from the body to life and sacred memory. We do respect the body. It is the instrument by which we know each other. God used human flesh for the incarnation. I was often asked as a pastor about the church's attitude toward cremation. My answer is that we are to afford the body respect but that its journey is over and many appropriate possibilities are open to us: cremation (which simply hastens the natural process of which the ritual speaks when it says, "Dust to dust, ashes to ashes"); willing the body to medicine for research; donating vital organs to the living; or burial where we return to the good earth, which nourishes us in life and receives us in death. Whatever the decision, make a respectful, loving disposition of the body; then turn to life, faith, and memory.

Third, we are to affirm our Christian faith that death is passing through a doorway from one kind of life to another. We have two worlds in which to develop understanding. First Peter reminds us that we have been born anew to a living hope through the resurrection of Jesus Christ from the dead. We came trailing clouds of glory from God and return to the same glory.

And finally, believe in the communion of saints. A mother said, after a child died, "One of the things I will miss is not having her to pray for." I replied, "Why not pray for her? You can continue to commend her to the love and mercy of God." We are surrounded by that invisible cloud of witnesses. And as we struggle to know what to do with all the new medical advances which confront us, ponder, pray, and make decisions in the context of a faith in the communion of saints.

We look into the future. What it holds, none can tell with certainty. But God will let light shine out of darkness. In 1772, the famous Quaker John Woolman wrote in his journal, "I have gone forward, not as one travelling in a road cast up and well-prepared, but as a man walking through a miry place in which are stones here and there safe to step on, but so situated that, one step being taken, time is necessary to see where to step next." We must take the next step. History cannot be reversed. But as we take those steps, let it be in the faith that has sustained us on our journey thus far.

9

Gambling

Newspaper articles of April 26, 1989, reported thousands of people flocking to Pennsylvania in search of the pot of gold at the end of the rainbow. That pot was Pennsylvania's Super 7 Lottery, swollen to a prize of more than $100 million. One article said there was pandemonium throughout the state, similar to sharks in a feeding frenzy.

Historically, The United Methodist Church has been opposed to gambling. In the days of the circuit riders, it was a struggle between the church and the forces represented by the saloon and gambling. Which would shape American life on the frontier? Card playing was viewed as an instrument of the devil for the destruction of the character of the emerging communities.

It's obvious gambling adds a sense of risk and excitement to life. Some parishioners once took me to the Kentucky Derby. It was one of the longest days of my life. We arrived about 9:00 in the morning and didn't leave until 6:00 in the evening. There were ten races. Each took about three minutes. The rest of the time the fans were to study the forms and place bets. Since I wasn't betting, I didn't have much to do except look at the horses and the crowd and wonder how much longer we had to wait before going home. Those betting, of course, were very interested in the outcome of each race.

It is impossible to take risk out of life. Those who buy stock take a risk. Almost any kind of investment involves a degree of uncertainty. Even banks and insurance companies have been going bankrupt.

But legalized gambling, from the United Methodist point of view, is destructive. The Social Principles, affirmed by the 1988 General Conference, include this statement:

Gambling is a menace to society, deadly to the best interests of moral, social, economic, and spiritual life, and destructive of good government. As an act of faith and love, Christians should abstain from gambling, and should strive to minister to those victimized by the practice. Where gambling has become addictive, the church will encourage such individuals to receive therapeutic assistance so that the individual's energies

83

may be redirected into positive and constructive ends. Community standards and personal lifestyles should be such as would make unnecessary and undesirable the resort to commercial gambling, including public lotteries, as a recreation, as an escape, or as a means of producing public revenue or funds for support of charities or government.[33]

I have found, however, that United Methodists have more than one opinion about gambling. During my years as bishop in Minnesota, the state voted on whether or not to have a lottery. Some parishioners wrote to me asking why we weren't more vigorous in opposing gambling. Others thought we should be more compassionate toward communities that were depressed as they searched for economic solutions, including the possibilities in gambling. I understood the frustration of both.

On one occasion, I asked pastors to survey their congregations in order to identify social issues they felt to be of major significance. On the subject of gambling, one pastor wrote: "My people do not think gambling is good for the compulsive gambler, but some of our people do make trips to Las Vegas and bingo parlors. A number of them bet on athletic events, and for some reason, in this highly churched state of Minnesota, we are going to pass a lottery bill."

A pastor once came and asked if I would resolve a conflict in her church. A group of ladies had made an unusually beautiful quilt. They wanted to raffle it off, saying they would realize more money for their United Methodist Women's mission budget than if it were sold at value. The pastor read the statement from the Social Principles to them, but they were not satisfied. I was not about to make the decision for the church. I did remind the pastor that the Social Principles are offered for our guidance. Since she had shared them with her parishioners, she could now let them struggle with the decision. I understand they decided to sell the quilt and not raffle it off.

In the summer of 1988, a United Methodist congregation in rural Minnesota turned down a $10,000 contribution from a service club in the small community of Ogilvie. This attracted national attention. The Lions Club had raised a large sum of money by sponsoring pull-tab gambling devices at local bars and restaurants. (People buy chances to pull back a tab in hopes that it will reveal they've won a jackpot.) Under state law, the Lions were required to give away a portion of their $146,106 profit. The club decided to present $10,000 each to the Roman Catholic, Missouri Synod Lutheran, United Methodist, and Christian Reformed congregations.

Three of the churches accepted the contribution, but the United Methodist congregation, after much discussion in the Administrative Board, declined the offer. Some wanted to take the money and do good with it. Others said if they took it, dissension might occur in the church as they tried to decide how to spend it. The congregation examined the Social Principles of the church which declare gambling of every kind to be "deadly to the best interests of moral, social, economic and spiritual life, and destructive of good government." Board members were asked to consider the implications of accepting money that may have been raised from people spending $100 on pull-tab gambling and not having enough money left to feed their families. After the decision was made, the pastor of the church said: "I think the community in general thinks we are crazy."

However, the editor of the *United Methodist Reporter* (Sept. 2, 1988) wrote:

> We support the premise that no form of gambling is "harmless." Hence, we commend the Ogilvie congregation's decision not to accept the gambling-generated $10,000 gift. But we don't assume the three churches who accepted similar gifts were acting as tools of the devil. They doubtless will find ways to use their gifts to "turn evil to good." If the church were to accept only gifts that could be certified 100% pure in their origin, many a good cause would be down the tubes. The remarkable thing about members of the Ogilvie congregation is their willingness to struggle with one another about an issue of right and wrong and then make a principled decision. In a day when cynics say that "everything and everyone has a price," it's encouraging to encounter a group of Christians who face temptation and decide: "Our convictions are not for sale."[34]

The editorial then asked: "What would you have done?" This question elicited a large number of letters. Some praised the small congregation for sticking to its principles, and others thought the church should have taken the money and used it for a worthy cause.

Scripture

What does the Bible say about gambling? There are few direct admonitions or guidelines. Gambling, "casting lots," was occasionally used as a way of making decisions. The Bible does have much to say, however, about the meaning and use of money. In general, prosperity is the blessing of the Old Testament and adversity of the New Testament. The Old Testament does have a line of thought that suggests the way to happiness is having neither too much nor too little. The wise person prays to God: "Give me neither poverty nor riches; or I shall be full, and deny you, and say, 'Who is the Lord?'" (Prov. 30:8). In other words, wealth is a secondary good. "A good name is to be chosen rather than great riches" (Prov. 22:1).

When we study Jesus' teaching about money, we note it is assumed the Christian will live an ordinary life. This means doing a job, earning pay, supporting those who are dependent on him or her. Paul was a qualified tradesman, and it was always his claim that wherever he stayed, he was a burden to no one, because he was self-supporting. He earned his money and paid his debts with his own work.

But there was great concern in the New Testament church that persons could become too fond of money. Hebrews 13:5 exhorts that the Christian is to keep life free from the love of money. We are not to put our trust in riches, for they are an insecure foundation. The value of life cannot be assessed by the size of one's wealth.

First Corinthians has an interesting verse: "On the first day of every week, each of you is to put aside and save whatever extra you earn, so that collections need not be taken when I come" (16:2). Paul is teaching that giving is to be systematic, proportionate, and universal—that is, everyone is to do it.

In commenting on this passage, William Barclay emphasizes that duty must not be the motive for this regular, systematic giving. In *The Letters to the Corinthians*, he writes: "A man never satisfies his Christian duty by discharging the obligations which he can legally be compelled to fulfill. . . . The really lovely thing is not something which is extracted from a man, however large it may be, but something which is given in the overflowing love of a man's heart, however small it may be." In other words, while Paul is encouraging regular giving, he wants it accepted as a Christian privilege. In the early church, almsgiving was an expression of one's faith, an evidence of righteousness. This may be why Jesus warned about the hazards of becoming wealthy. Perhaps there is something inherently evil in money. Why did he say a rich man would have difficulty entering the kingdom (Matt. 19:24)?

Martin Luther came up with an answer when he explained the Tenth Commandment in the Large Catechism: "What is it to have a god? What is God? A god is that to which we look for all good and in which we find refuge in every time of need. Many a person thinks he has God and everything he needs when he has money and property; in them he trusts and of them he boasts so stubbornly and securely that he cares for no one." In other words, addiction to a "money standard" of life destroys a relationship of trust toward God and results in anxiety and insecurity.

Materialism

Studies have shown that a prime motivation for gambling is the hope of gaining enough money to be comfortable without having to work. But is it biblical to hope to get through life without working? Paul told the Thessalonians that he who doesn't work shouldn't eat (2 Thess. 3:10).

Our problem as Americans is probably not materialism. We are no more materialistic than other people. The people who have the least may be most concerned about things. We are not a selfish people. By and large, the American people are generous when convinced of the importance of a need. We are touched by suffering, and we do give of ourselves. We are a nation of volunteers. But if neither materialism nor selfishness is the issue, what is it? It is idolatry. It is assuming money can solve all problems and is the goal of all our striving. We are willing to "sell all we have" (relationships, faith, a life-affirming way of living) for the pearl of great price which is money! Jesus said to the rich young man, "Get rid of all your wealth and follow me" and in that moment the rich young man sorrowfully discovered his god. This is the problem of gambling. We are selling much of great value in order to satisfy the god of money.

Ted Koppel, a television news personality, in a widely acclaimed address at a college, said that the tablets Moses brought from Mount Sinai were not the "Ten Suggestions." He said that the brilliance of the Commandments is that in very few words they convey standards of acceptable human behavior. Koppel then discussed the relevance of some of these commandments for our complex society. He pointed out that the tenth commandment seems particularly relevant to the current pervasive covetous attitude, warning against dishonest or illegal gain.

Lotteries

Perhaps the tenth commandment does have something to say about gambling, lotteries, and our hope of instant riches. Florida is the state most heavily involved in gambling. In its first year, the Florida lottery sold $128 worth of tickets for every man, woman, and child in the state. Yet interviews of ticket retailers confirm what surveys have shown: Most tickets are purchased by a relatively small group of heavy players. The *Christian Science Monitor* reported that state officials are concerned that money from the lottery replaces rather than supplements educational funding.

On a long-term, practical level, how educational can it be for children to watch hardworking parents and other adults either lose or profit from chance-taking? Is provision for education and other important programs in a state to be dependent upon a matter of chance? Is it necessary for many to lose so that a few may profit?

Studies show that approximately one-half of our teenagers have gambled within the last year. Questions need to be asked about the effect of lotteries. They form a gateway to other kinds of gambling. The executive director of the National Council on Compulsive Gambling believes that information on gambling disorders should be taught in schools—alongside programs about alcohol and other drugs.

Compulsive Gambling

The promotion of lotteries is handled in a manner similar to the way smoking used to be glamorized. It doesn't show the down side. Ads never show persons who lose a home or become severely depressed over the financial problems that result from gambling more than they could afford. While most people have personal limits on the amount they will bet, more than 3 percent of the adult population have serious problems. They are compulsive gamblers. Lotteries create a new and readily available route to disaster for them.

In *Psychology Today,* December 1985, Alexander P. Blaszczynski said that the number of people who gamble generally depends upon the availability of gambling outlets. As opportunities expand, more people gamble and the number of actual and potential pathological gamblers increases. He recommends that society restrict gambling outlets and that we educate high school students about the dangers of excessive gambling. Drawing lessons from the Prohibition Era, he does not think gambling should be totally suppressed. It should be controlled through social reform and education, not prohibition.

Even if we do good with the earnings from gambling, Christians must ask pointed questions. Is it biblical to rely on luck as a way out of poverty or to ensure we will never have to work again? Is it right to profit from something at the expense of others? Winnings come from the losses experienced by others. Are we caring for our fellow human beings by encouraging them to gamble?

A Christian Response

I was discussing this issue with a small group of laypersons in a local church. One of them, who has gone to General Conference, said that it was her observation that we pass resolutions on gambling at General Conference and it makes us feel good, but then we don't do anything about it afterward. However, there are instances where we are trying. Many of our annual conferences have invested heavily in leading campaigns to resist the establishment of the lottery system. The craze to get in on the so-called easy money is such that rarely have we been successful in defeating gambling proposals, but as a denomination we do take gambling seriously. In 1988 the Virginia Annual Conference invested $58,000 to defeat a proposition that would permit a local option on parimutuel betting. Thirteen percent of the resolutions passed by our annual conferences in 1988 registered opposition to gambling.

This concern is not new. For centuries Christians believed gambling to be wrong. In A.D. 306 the Ecclesiastical Council of Elvira prescribed a year of public penance for any Catholic involved in a game of chance. Today many Christians still believe gambling to be wrong. There are reasons for this. The first has to do with being a good steward of our time and of our money. More basic to Christians is the *philosophy* of gambling. Why do people gamble? Some do it for excitement and entertainment. The director of a state lottery was quoted in a news article as saying that people play because it is fun. Even if you don't win, there is some excitement as you await the outcome. A pastor in Pennsylvania asked a woman why she bought a dollar lottery ticket every day and her response was, "A dollar isn't very much for twenty-four hours of hope."

As Christians our hope is not founded in "luck" but in what God has done for us through Jesus Christ. As we are reminded in scripture: "He has given us a new birth into a living hope through the resurrection of Jesus Christ from the dead" (1 Pet. 1:3).

The Bible tells us plainly that God not only *is* but *is eternal*. God is almighty, unchanging. God cares for what has been created and this includes each person. In Proverbs 10:22 we read: "The blessing of the Lord makes rich," and in Psalm 23:1 "The Lord is my shepherd, I shall not want."

It is easier to say this than to prove it. For many people, circumstances are tough and there is apparently little reason for hope. Yet there is a law of God that supersedes the supposed force of circumstance. There is a spiritual reality that affirms God's absolute supremacy and our inseparability from that care. We are made in the divine image and, therefore, we receive love and care. Paul records in Romans 8:28, "We know that all things work together for good for those who love God, who are called according to his purpose." And in Philippians he writes to the first congregation established in European soil saying, "I want you to know, beloved, that what has happened to me has actually helped to spread the gospel" (1:12).

Risk Taking for a Cause

Risk taking for a worthy cause reveals humanity at its noblest. G. A. Studdert-Kennedy wrote a poem indicating that Jesus gambled, even as the soldiers who waited at the foot of the cross and rolled the dice to see which one would get the rumpled, bloodstained, seamless robe that Jesus had worn. The poem is titled "He Was a Gambler Too."

> And, sitting down, they watched Him there,
> The soldiers did;
> There, while they played with dice,
> He made His Sacrifice,
> And died upon the Cross to rid
> God's world of sin.
> He was a gambler, too, my Christ,
> He took His life and threw
> It for a world redeemed.
> And ere His agony was done,
> Before the westering sun went down,
> Crowning that day with its crimson crown,
> He knew that He had won.[35]

In *Signs of Our Times* William K. Quick asserts that "Jesus gambled. Not in the sense of the soldiers or Pilate or Caiaphas. He gambled for higher stakes. He risked everything in his faithfulness to the Father. . . . On Calvary Jesus gambled for love against hate, and he won."

Money is an important possession because each of us barters some of our life in exchange for it. Ours is a monetary society and, while money does not have the power to solve all problems, it can make a sizable dent in some of them. Money is power because it commands resources. Lack of money can limit freedom, for we cannot choose where or how we will live.

Money is important. It can be squandered or given to benevolent causes. It can buy luxuries or build schools and churches. It can maintain an opulent lifestyle or provide food and shelter for persons in need. As Christians we take seriously the use of whatever money we have. The Bible reminds us to be good and faithful stewards (Luke 16:2). Gambling involves risk taken for selfish gain at the expense of others. From the United Methodist perspective, that sums it up and is the reason we conclude that all gambling is destructive of the strength of democracy and contrary to the highest values of the Judeo-Christian tradition.

10

Capital Punishment

In a previous chapter, we examined the church's attitude on abortion. Out of that discussion emerges an interesting question. If you are pro-life, does that have other implications? Bishop Lowell Erdahl, a Lutheran bishop, in a book titled *Pro-Life/Pro-Peace* is pro-life and proud of it. He doesn't support abortion, but neither does he support nuclear war, mercy killing, or capital punishment. He wants legislation that says no one has the right to take life at any stage of development. He wishes the civil laws said it is never permissible to kill except in tragic, exceptional circumstances. He goes after all the life issues and sees that they are related.

It may be that Bishop Erdahl is more consistent than The United Methodist Church or either of the political parties. The platform of the Republican Party in 1988 was anti-abortion but in favor of the establishment of the federal death penalty. The Democratic Party platform avoided the issue of capital punishment but supported a woman's choice in abortion. The United Methodist Church, which would permit abortion under certain circumstances, says "we oppose capital punishment and urge its elimination from all criminal codes."

This statement comes at the end of a rather long paragraph in *The Book of Discipline:*

> To protect all citizens from those who would encroach upon personal and property rights, it is the duty of governments to establish police forces, courts, and facilities for the confinement, punishment, and rehabilitation of offenders. We support governmental measures designed to reduce and eliminate crime, consistent with respect for the basic freedom of persons. . . . In the love of Christ who came to save those who are lost and vulnerable, we urge the creation of genuinely new systems for the care and support of victims of crime and for rehabilitation that will restore, preserve, and nurture the humanity of the imprisoned. For the same reason, we oppose capital punishment and urge its elimination from all criminal codes.[36]

Intellectually, I agree with this last sentence. Emotionally, I sometimes waver. A young woman, a member of a congregation I served as pastor, was abducted while entering her car at a shopping mall. Days later her body was found in an abandoned barn. She had been bound, tortured, and raped before being killed. Some months later a serial killer confessed to the murder. Knowing this fine young woman, her husband, and her family personalized the crime for me. As I imagined her terror and physical suffering at the time of her death, something within me called for revenge. I suspect most of us feel this way on occasion.

Yet, the church has consistently spoken out against capital punishment. In the 1980 session of the General Conference a resolution was adopted which said in part:

> After a moratorium of a full decade, the use of the death penalty in the United States has resumed. Other Western nations have largely abolished it during the 20th century. But a rapidly rising rate of crime and an even greater increase in the fear of crime has generated support within the American society for the institution of death as the punishment for certain forms of homicide. It is now being asserted, as it was often in the past, that capital punishment would deter criminals and would protect law-abiding citizens. . . .
>
> The United Methodist Church cannot accept retribution or social vengeance as a reason for taking human life. It violates our deepest belief in God as the creator and the redeemer of humankind. In this respect, there can be no assertion that human life can be taken humanely by the state. Indeed, in the long run, the use of the death penalty by the state will increase the acceptance of revenge in our society and will give official sanction to a climate of violence. . . .
>
> The death penalty also falls unfairly and unequally upon an outcast minority. Recent methods for selecting the few persons sentenced to die from among the larger number who are convicted of comparable offenses have not cured the arbitrariness and discrimination that have historically marked the administration of capital punishment in this country.[37]

The 1984 General Conference adopted a resolution which included these additional concepts:

> Whereas, we believe the state cannot teach respect for human life by destroying human life; and Whereas, the Holy Scriptures teach us that human life is both sacred and divine and that we bear the image of the incorruptible God; and Whereas, Jesus Christ taught us love, forgiveness and reconciliation; and Whereas, all Christians are under divine mandate to safeguard life and work for the salvation of all humankind; *Therefore be it resolved*, that The United Methodist Church reaffirm strongly its position against capital punishment.[38]

Scripture

Lloyd Bailey, a professor at Duke University, has written a book titled *Capital Punishment: What the Bible Says*. He begins with a story out of his childhood about a murder trial. The prosecutor, knowing most of the jurors were people of faith, reminded them the Bible teaches: "Thou shalt not kill" (Exod. 20:13, KJV). The defendant had broken not only the laws of the state but of God. The defense attorney, seeking to reverse the thrust of the biblical injunction, pointed out that, after all, execution was itself a form of killing. The commandment, then, should prevent the jurors from convicting the defendant of murder. To do so would be a violation of the Bible.

Both those who advocate capital punishment and those who oppose it resort to the Bible. Capital punishment was sanctioned by the society out of which the Hebrew Bible (Old Testament) grew. The first five books of the Bible list at least seventeen offenses for which a person may die. Some, such as "contempt for parents" or "trespass upon sacred areas or things," seem rather trivial. One reason Hebrew society used capital punishment was deterrence. "All the people will hear and be afraid, and will not act presumptuously again" (Duet. 17:13). This is one of the reasons we hear today for using the death penalty: "We want to send a message."

Bailey, after an exhaustive examination of biblical texts, concludes: "For those who desire to bring a theological perspective to the contemporary debate about capital punishment for murder, there is a large amount of biblical data to which one may turn for information or guidance. That evidence uniformly authorizes the penalty of death for murder in Israel, but it is within the context of the certainty of guilt and equality before the law."[39] The author questions whether we should sanction capital punishment on biblical grounds without also demanding its attendant safeguards. There had to be certainty of guilt. We have executed persons on the basis of circumstantial evidence. We also know eyewitnesses are not totally trustworthy. Two people observing the same incident will describe it differently. A second standard in biblical jurisprudence was that the socioeconomic status of the accused would have no bearing upon the verdict. In the United States, however, as Mr. Bailey observes:

> One's chances of being convicted, sentenced to die, and actually executed are apparently related to one's sex, race, and income. Indeed, in 1972 the U.S. Supreme Court ruled that under existing laws execution was so "harsh, freakish, and arbitrary" that is constituted "cruel and unusual punishment in violation of the Eighth and Fourteenth Amendments."

In sum: although there is no biblical basis for objection to the death penalty per se, the divergences between Israelite society and our own raise very serious questions with which Church and Synagogue must struggle.[40]

As I see it, the Bible does not lay a mandate on modern states to exercise capital punishment, but it does permit it. The general tenor of scripture, however, seems to suggest that capital punishment is prudently exercised only under extreme conditions and not as a general rule.

Public Opinion

In a 1981 ABC News-*Washington Post* poll on why people oppose or support the death penalty for those convicted of murder, opponents cited as their three top reasons: "Taking a second life will not solve anything"; "religion forbids it—the Bible says 'thou shalt not kill'"; and "the legal system is not equitable." Proponents of capital punishment gave as their top reasons for support: "Revenge—an eye for an eye"; "it's a crime deterrent"; and "jail does not rehabilitate—murderers may get paroled and do it again."

It is obvious that United Methodists—and Americans in general—are divided on this matter. Both sides are able to marshall arguments supporting their position. Note the varied responses to the execution of mass murderer Ted Bundy in January 1989. On television he came across as a thoroughly winsome young man, the antithesis of the menacing figures we assume populate death row. But he seemed driven by uncontrollable impulses to kill in order to achieve a "high" on excitement. He was convicted of raping and killing a twelve-year-old girl. The press estimated, however, that he may have killed as many as a hundred persons. First sentenced in 1979, the former law student spent ten years delaying his execution with legal maneuvers. During that time he showed no contrition. Some people celebrated his execution.

Syndicated columnist Patrick Buchanan, in an article published the week of January 29, 1989, commended the 2,000 who gathered to cheer the death of Ted Bundy. He suggested that they were behaving naturally upon seeing justice carried out. He supported them for acting on the religious concept that we are rational beings with a knowledge of right and wrong and the free will to choose either. In connection with this, Buchanan believes the state has power to protect society and to punish evil-doers. We do differ in our opinions as to what should be done with criminals such as Bundy.

Let us now examine some of the arguments that support the United Methodist position. First, capital punishment as a deterrent is questionable. The deterrent value is a hotly debated point. Let's acknowledge that statistics can be advanced to support both sides. Deterrence, however, requires would-be murderers to reckon with the probable costs of their actions, a rational assessment unlikely to be made by those drunk, high on drugs, or in fits of anger. And the United States seems unwilling to execute in numbers sufficient to impress calculating killers. Even in the peak year of 1933, the 199 who were executed represented a scant 2 percent of all murderers convicted. In other words, so many avoid the death penalty that it has lost much of its value as a deterrent to crime.

In Washington, DC alone, there are 1.7 killings every day. If everyone who commits murder is to be executed, our legal system as constituted is totally incapable of fulfilling the assignment. Nationally, it would mean dozens of executions on a daily basis.

Second, capital punishment in this country is not equitably administered. Sometimes individuals involved in the same crime receive totally different sentences. Charles Brooks was killed by lethal injection on December 7, 1982, in Texas for the murder of a garage attendant during a robbery. His accomplice, who may actually have pulled the trigger, could be eligible for parole within a few years because of a technicality in the jury-selection process.

Furthermore, the poor can't afford the same legal defense as the rich. Public defenders are overburdened and do not have the time or resources to handle the complexities of capital cases.

Third, one of the most serious charges against the death penalty is that it is irreversible, and an innocent person could die. Quoted in *Christianity Today* (March 2, 1984), Judge Harry Fogle reflects: "I've seen four people convicted of first-degree murder, sentenced to the chair, and later saved by confessions of those who actually committed the crime. The idea that human beings can decide who should live and die is specious. In the last hundred years we've had a hundred mistakes in capital cases. One is too many, and we've averaged one a year."[41]

Fourth is the fact that the United States is the only Western industrial nation still practicing the death penalty in peacetime. This makes us wonder if we are projecting the image that we wish.

Jeff Greenfield, a syndicated columnist and commentator for ABC News, in a column published January 28, 1989, wrote that few people could really say it was wrong to execute Ted Bundy, the handsome, personable, bright man who killed and mutilated for fun. Yet Greenfield argues that there is still one reality that ought to give even the most fervent supporter of capital punishment a moment of pause: Why do almost all free societies save ours ban the death penalty, while every dictatorship uses it enthusiastically?

A popular slogan of abolitionists reads, "Why do we kill people who kill people, to teach that killing people is wrong?" Greenfield points out that this is paradoxical. The severity of a punishment for doing wrong may be the best way possible to show how highly we hold the value that has been betrayed by the wrongdoer: the value of life.

Fifth, birth and death belong to God. George Boyd in a provocative *Christian Century* article (Feb. 17, 1988) acknowledged that capital punishment is often deserved. Many convicted criminals morally deserve execution. A person voluntarily taking another's life forfeits any claim that society should respect the murderer's life. Murderers, according to Boyd, deserve no better fate than that of their victims. The issue, however, is not what the criminals have done or deserve, but what society should do and be in response.

Execution may be deserved, but there are strong arguments for discontinuing the death penalty. Says Boyd:

> The most fundamental argument for discontinuing the death penalty is that society can best express the seriousness of its commitment to the sanctity of human life by abstaining from taking it, despite having justifiable cause. To respect human life precisely where its bearer has forfeited personal claim to that respect would be society's ultimate statement both of the sanctity of life and of the kind of society it wants to be. . . . Murderers should never be allowed the comfort of the illusion that they can "pay" for their crime.[42]

Boyd looks at one more argument. He does not think that the possibility of a mistake or the deterrence theory or the capacity of society to protect itself equally well by permanently imprisoning those who are currently being executed are of ultimate importance in making a decision as to whether or not society should use capital punishment. The *final* argument, he says, was set forth by a ranking member of Pat Robertson's presidential campaign when he said that he opposed capital punishment on the grounds that responsibility for life and death belongs to God!

What of the Future?

Marshall Shelley (*Christianity Today*, March 2, 1984) wonders about the future of the death penalty. He believes that it is unlikely that the death penalty will be abolished in the United States anytime soon. Juries and judges will continue having to make life-and-death decisions. He observes that passing judgment is not an enjoyable experience for a juror. Even when guilt is not in question, justice can't make up for a wrong. Until God administers absolute justice, God has given us the responsibility of passing judgment.

As I work through the various arguments on both sides of this complex issue, I find compelling reasons for both positions, Greed, hate, and sexual passion are at the base of most murders. I'm not sure that capital punishment would be much of a deterrent to a person caught up in one of these motives. Similarly, emotion is often the reason for wishing to impose the death penalty. When particularly gruesome crimes are committed, we react at the visceral level with fear, disgust, and a feeling that the culprit doesn't deserve to live.

When I am trying to live at the level of the rational and the reasonable or put into practice the high moral concepts of the Christian faith, then I doubt the wisdom of capital punishment and conclude the General Conference is right when it calls for the elimination of this practice as something that debases human society, does not make us safer or more just, and commits us to the downward spiral of ever-increasing violence. As I write these words, I am dispassionate. It is possible for me to conclude that the practice of capital punishment does not belong in a society that holds itself to be "under God" and professes to be the most progressive and compassionate on the face of the earth. But when I remember what a criminal did to a young woman parishioner, murdering her with deliberate cruelty, something visceral again calls out for revenge. It is then that I must remember the words of scripture: "Vengeance is mine, saith the Lord."

11

Peace

If you were to ask any gathering of United Methodists, "Are you in favor of peace?," every head would nod. I do not know anyone who prefers war to peace. What divides us is how to achieve and maintain it. In the Social Principles of our denomination there is a paragraph titled "War and Peace."

We believe war is incompatible with the teachings and example of Christ. We therefore reject war as an instrument of national foreign policy and insist that the first moral duty of all nations is to resolve by peaceful means every dispute that arises between or among them; that human values must outweigh military claims as governments determine their priorities; that the militarization of society must be challenged and stopped; that the manufacture, sale, and deployment of armaments must be reduced and controlled; and that the production, possession, or use of nuclear weapons be condemned.[43]

This comprehensive, far-reaching statement has many implications. If we reject war as an instrument of foreign policy, what do we put in its place? Every thoughtful person condemns nuclear weapons, but how do you get the genie back in the bottle? There have been five historical manifestations of group Christian pacifism. There were the early Christians in the first three centuries; then a variety of sects in the Middle Ages; the Swiss Anabaptists and Dutch Mennonites in the sixteenth century; the English Quakers in the seventeenth century; and, last, in the present, the historic peace denominations as well as a few of the conciliar organizations. All of these expressions have had value as they contribute to the effort to accomplish peace. Furthermore, they stand as a constant challenge to nations and leaders to work toward alternatives to war. Each group has built on the foundations laid by those who went before, accepting earlier perceptions or arguments and adding something of their own. It is our responsibility to do the same.

The United Methodist Church, while greatly concerned about peace, has never been identified as one of the historic peace denominations as have the Mennonites or the Quakers. But we have had a strong interest in working for peace; and the General Conference, through the years, has issued many resolutions on the subject. But do moral injunctions and biblical exhortations have much to say to national policy? I might, as an individual, practice pacifism, but can "turn the other cheek" become a cornerstone of national policy? Probably not.

Let's briefly examine some of our recent presidents. Richard Nixon, who was reared in a Quaker tradition, had a law degree from a United Methodist institution, held religious services in the White House as a symbol of a nation under God, demonstrated strong family loyalty and commitment, and said on national television, "Your president will never lie to you," did, in fact, lie to us. As one revelation followed another, the American people were dismayed that the administration had been lacking in plain, old-fashioned truth and honesty. The remarkable achievements of the Nixon Administration were forgotten as the people rose up and drove him from office—not because someone on his committee was guilty of breaking and entering but because trust was gone. We had been betrayed.

Gerald Ford then entered the Oval Office. To most people, he came across as a sincere man, a good man. In another time he would probably have been elected to a full term. But he bore the onus of being a part of the Nixon Administration, and there was a suspicion, after the quick pardon, that there had been a deal. This was a handicap he could not overcome.

There were many presidential candidates in 1976, but when the final vote was counted, we had elected someone outside the Washington establishment, someone from the soil, a farmer, someone who was an evangelical, born-again Southern Baptist, who taught a Sunday school class and regularly went to church. Now, we said to ourselves, we will have a moral president, as we deserve, for we are proud of the fact that our Pledge of Allegiance affirms that we are a nation "under God," with a Puritan heritage, where the freedom to worship according to the dictates of our own conscience is the bedrock of our freedoms.

Although Jimmy Carter had served as governor of Georgia, in the judgment of many political analysts he was the least qualified candidate in terms of experience and background. He was elected because we believed somehow that he would restore decency, integrity, and morality—and give us a government as good as we sincerely believe we are. But after some years in the office, the nation reluctantly concluded that being a good man does not necessarily qualify a person to be an effective president. More than one columnist wrote that if Carter were to succeed as president, he

would have to fail as a Christian. Public opinion polls of that period
reflected a high degree of confidence in his character but rated the
president low in terms of effectiveness.

I cite this example not from the point of view of any political bias,
for that is not my intent. Rather, it is to suggest that at least from
the perspective of conventional wisdom, basing foreign policy on
traditional Christian principles may not be the most effective thing
to do. Still, we do believe that a nation such as ours can and must
shape policy according to an overarching concept of what is right
and good and by a conscious attempt to express that in international relationships. If we are a moral nation, then our policies
should be girded by imperatives that grow out of the nature of
God, principles of truth, and the ideals of decency.

But let's be clear: Being moral does not mean being naive. I grew
up in a time when the high-minded and utopian dreams of pacifism
for the world were shattered by Hitler's blitzkrieg. Pacifism will not
lead to peace for all. Those who take sin seriously would never make
the mistake of believing that in the first place. The nonviolence of
Christ did not prevent him from being hanged on the cross. Loving
our enemies does not ensure they will become our friends.

The *individual* may follow the commands of Christ to their ultimate conclusion. The *individual* may say there will be no compromise with the world that bows to the dictates of violence and
revenge. The *individual* may condemn any use of force. But *society*
is required to realize that evil must be restrained and society will, if
necessary, use force even when aware of its ultimate futility.

Sojourner magazine carried an article about Ron Coleman, who
became a missile launch officer in command of the crew in a missile
silo. He was one of two people assigned to turn the key that would
send the missile on its fiery journey if the order were handed down
to launch U.S. intercontinental nuclear missiles. Officers in missile
silos carry a pistol in a hip holster. They are under orders to shoot if
another officer fails to obey the command to turn the key. In an
interview later, Coleman admitted that he felt "virtually certain" he
would refuse to turn the key if the missile were targeted on a large
city. He had become involved in a study group at his church. He
began to feel tension mounting between his faith and his work.
Finally, he decided to end his military career. He explained to a
colleague that he felt that what he was doing was no longer compat-
ible with his faith. There were significant consequences as a result of
his decision. Family income was reduced by over one-half. His new
job was not particularly satisfying. Yet he said he had no regrets.

I cite this example to show that individuals are compelled to
make personal decisions on the basis of principles that cannot

necessarily become national policy. National policy will recognize the complexity of issues and will acknowledge that judgments must be made between less-than-perfect alternatives. In the Christmas 1987 issue of *USA Today,* the editor wrote:

> War is a blight on civilized society. Those who argue that it has given us scientific miracles, jobs and progress turn their backs on the fact that it has robbed the world of human life with all its potential for genius and brilliance. The way to progress in this world—the only way—is for national leaders and world powers to end the arms race, to halt the sale of weapons of war, to adopt methods of diplomacy, to replace the instinct for war.[44]

Another viewpoint is the world will never be at peace, but even if it were, problems would abound. First, the economy would be a mess as persons in the armed forces and those who work in defense industries would be jobless. Also, many discoveries and inventions that come about from necessity due to war will be eliminated or slowed down.

Obviously, we reject this cold-blooded pragmatism. We know there will be a constant struggle for power. We know jealousy and selfishness are prevalent. But we must dream, work, and plan for a day when we will start treating each other as brothers and sisters. We know good intentions will not suffice. Neither can we cynically surrender to the idea that there will always be "war and rumors of war" and there is nothing we can do except yield to the inevitable. We are created to dream of and work for a world that is better, a world where innocent people are not killed, where the best of our youth are not sent off to be killed, where our resources are no longer poured into the machines of war but into making life a little richer and more complete for all persons.

A college student stopped by my office to talk with me about his experiences on campus. He mentioned that he had taken a course on the American presidents. I raised with him the question as to whether a moral presidency is possible. His response was superb. He said, "You cannot have a moral presidency unless you have a moral people to back it up." Perhaps that says it all. In the long journey of history, a nation cannot survive without an overarching sense of right and wrong to guide the decision-making process.

Conscientious Objection

While going through some old papers recently, I came across my draft registration card issued in 1941. Shortly before World War II, Congress established the draft. I was "4-F" because I was in theological school, studying for the ministry, and as a seminarian was exempt from military conscription. Congress also recognized that there were persons who, while not clergy, conscientiously objected to bearing arms. Those who were members of churches that had a history of being "peace" denominations such as the Mennonites were usually regarded as being authentic objectors. Others had a more difficult time convincing a draft board as to the genuineness of their objection. Those with the status of "objector" during World War II were usually given alternative assignments, some of which were highly dangerous, such as working as a stretcher bearer on the battlefield.

The General Conference in 1988 affirmed a long-standing position of our denomination when it said:

> The United Methodist Church supports all persons who make decisions of conscience in regard to military service. The ministry of the church is not limited to those who conscientiously serve in the armed forces of their nation. It is also extended to those who, as a matter of conscience, refuse to serve in the armed forces, to cooperate with systems of military conscription, or to accept alternative service.[45]

The history of our nation clearly favors this posture. In 1814 Representative Daniel Webster asked: "Where is it written into the Constitution . . . that you may take children from their parents, and parents from their children, and compel them to fight the battles of any war, in which the folly or wickedness of Government may engage it?" During American history, conscription has been in effect for only forty years, less than 17 percent of the time. Of those years, only thirteen were during peacetime.

The fear of losses in political and religious freedom resulting from large standing armies was one of the underlying themes of the Declaration of Independence and the Constitution. George Washington had to rely almost entirely on volunteers to wage the War of Independence. During the debate over ratification of the Constitution, one argument held that having armies during peace time endangered liberty and therefore should be avoided if possible.

The issue of conscription was raised at the time of the War of 1812 but was not implemented. At the time of the Civil War it was again established with significant modifications. In World War I and World War II the draft was used. Following Pearl Harbor and our formal entry into the war, general opposition diminished. As part of the demobilization following the war, the draft act was allowed to expire. However, with the Cold War gaining the headlines, a peacetime draft bill was passed in 1948 and was kept in place through the Vietnam era. There was, however, widespread opposition. During the Vietnam War, over 200,000 cases were referred to the Justice Department by Selective Service officials for various violations. It is estimated that over 250,000 men failed to register and were never prosecuted, and approximately 60,000 men went into exile in Canada and Europe. Thousands of draft files were burned, bloodied, or destroyed. On one day—June 10, 1970—12,000 men publicly burned their draft cards. Many persons sought alternatives to going to Vietnam by enrolling in the National Guard, although there was no guarantee the Guard would not be called to active duty. Others sought assignment to inner-city service and other noncombat arenas. On January 27, 1973, the Paris Peace Agreement was signed. Immediately thereafter, Secretary of Defense Melvin Laird stated: "I wish to inform you that the Armed Forces henceforth will depend exclusively on volunteer soldiers, sailors, airmen, and Marines. Use of the draft has ended."

In various statements the General Conference has opposed peacetime conscription. There are valid reasons for this position. It is a massive tax drain to support the bureaucracy of such massive undertakings. The opportunity for indoctrination poses a threat to peace and freedom. And obviously, there is an invasion of personal liberty and privacy. The church makes it clear that its opposition is reserved for peacetime periods but does call on United Methodists to work for the elimination of conscription systems in times other than those of war or national emergency.

Following Vietnam, there was an effort to declare an amnesty for those who had evaded the draft. In many ways, that seemed very unfair. Of those who responded to the draft, over 50,000 were killed and hundreds of thousands wounded. Why should others be permitted to go free? The draft during Vietnam, of course, was very selective. Those in college were deferred. Those from homes of affluence often could find alternative kinds of service. The burden fell very unfairly on the poor and those without the intellectual or financial capabilities for attending college. (Following the Persian Gulf War, there was also a proposal to declare a general amnesty for those troops, few in number, who refused to engage in combat duty. At the time of this writing, the issue was not resolved.)

To ignore the fact that the law had been broken by the resisters and "draft dodgers" would be to ignore the sacrifice of thousands of loyal young Americans who did so much. Yet many of the resisters were saying, "We cannot participate in a war which we consider to be immoral and unjust."

The United Methodist Church recognized the dilemma the young men encountered. Either they faced being wounded and killed, or they had to make an agonizing decision of conscience to separate from the war. Therefore, The United Methodist Church argued for a general amnesty, suggesting that a government that is concerned to heal the wounds of war and rectify injustice will probably inspire a higher morale than a government that seeks the last drop of blood from every citizen. Recognizing the right of conscience is one way a nation can bind up the wounds, heal the divisions, and set the feet of its people on the path of peace.

The 1988 *Book of Discipline* (para. 74) states:

> We reject national policies of enforced military service as incompatible with the gospel. We acknowledge the agonizing tension created by the demand for military service by national Church as they reach a conscientious decision concerning the nature of their responsibility as citizens. Pastors are called upon to be available for counseling with all young adults who face conscription, including those who conscientiously refuse to cooperate with a system of conscription.
>
> We support and extend the ministry of the Church to those persons who conscientiously oppose all war, or any particular war, and who therefore refuse to serve in the armed forces or to cooperate with systems of military conscription. We also support and extend the Church's ministry to those persons who conscientiously choose to serve in the armed forces or to accept alternative service.

Nuclear Weapons

In the mid-Eighties, my wife and I conducted overseas retreats for military chaplains and their families. We visited bases and posts, observing the settings in which ministry takes place. Many of these are very stressful situations. We spent a day on the border between East and West Germany where tensions were, at that time, very high. This was before the amazing events of 1989-90 which saw the fall of the Berlin Wall. Our chaplain there took us to visit the Commander of the Third Division, who had previously taught political science at West Point. We spent two hours with him. He was articulate, informed, and concerned. He said, "Should the Warsaw Pact nations attack, we could withstand them for two weeks with conventional weapons. The French have said that, should the enemy reach the Rhine, they would shoot nuclear bombs. Nuclear bombs," he said, "act as a deterrent assuring there will be no attack." He then continued, "I hate nuclear weapons. I hate spending my life out here in the muck on the front lines. But what can we do? The fact that we have deterrent weapons means that no country in Europe has been shooting at another country for forty years. That's the longest period in the history of Europe that someone has not been shooting at another person. It's not peace, but at least human lives are not being destroyed."

This commander indicated why our government has a commitment to nuclear weapons, even after the fall of the Berlin Wall and other events heralding the spread of democracy in Eastern Europe. It is "cheap" defense. We do not have sufficient conventional weapons to win a traditional war in Europe, nor would our people be willing to pay the taxes required to maintain a conventional army of the size necessary to fight a conventional war. We rely on nuclear weaponry. But it is a terrible thing to know we are all hostages to this monster that can destroy not only human life but God's created order. MAD (Mutually Assured Destruction) has kept us from using nuclear weapons. Yet it is untenable that our youth should grow up wondering if they will have a future or whether this beautiful earth will be destroyed through the folly or mistakes of our leaders.

I do believe all nuclear weapons must finally be removed. This will not of itself bring peace. In the latter part of the Eighties, fifty nations were involved in war or were battling insurgents. Thousands were being killed each month. But nuclear weapons could destroy not only human life but all of creation. Their removal would not mean we no longer have war. It would mean that the human race and this earth might have a chance to survive.

In April 1986, the Council of Bishops issued a pastoral letter to The United Methodist Church which they titled "In Defense of Creation." There was lively and spirited debate in the Council. There were disagreements about the wording of some paragraphs. There was unanimity, however, in the conviction that everyone should do all that is possible to eliminate nuclear weapons. Interest in this subject was evidenced by the fact that all the major television networks had representatives at the Council meeting. The day following the adoption of the document, the news broke concerning the nuclear crisis at Chernobyl, one of the power plants in Russia. It dramatized how nuclear proliferation jeopardizes the earth.

Military Personnel

I wish to add a personal observation about those who serve in the military. During World War II the uniform commanded great respect. But during the Vietnam era, those who were in uniform often felt obligated to apologize for it. The individual Christian pacifist believes that Christ's commands in the Sermon on the Mount and the larger spirit of love which Christ taught and exemplified require that one stand ready to suffer and die at the hands of our nation's enemies but forbid one to participate in war. But national policy says that the United States is morally as well as legally obligated to maintain a military defense of this imperfect nation in an imperfect world. I do not, therefore, look on those who serve in the military as misguided. They are fulfilling a calling and a mission. As I visited more than a dozen military installations in five different countries, I developed a profound respect for the dedication of those who serve in the defense of the country. On one occasion I received a letter from a chaplain who was from the conference where I was serving as bishop. He said:

> The people with whom I work are not the bumbling idiots who make war for the sake of trying out new weaponry as is so often depicted by television and motion pictures. "Rambo" is the hero of no one that I know. Quite to the contrary, my military colleagues are good, honest, sincere, and dedicated folks. A cross-section of personnel from the Pentagon would not be unlike a cross-section of any congregation of United Methodists.

I expect he is right. At least, that conforms to my experience. So when the Bishops' pastoral letter speaks of the horrors of nuclear weaponry, it is not criticizing those who serve the country in the military. It is saying that the human race must seek ways of removing the weapons we now have that could totally destroy both the human race and our planet earth. The United Methodist Church, in its peace pronouncements, is speaking against no one. It is speaking in "Defense of God's Creation."

The Arms Race

Recent administrations in our nation have endeavored to enter into negotiations with the Russians in an effort to slow down the arms race and remove certain categories of weapons. This has resulted in bitter political fighting. Many feel that unless we have nuclear superiority, our own national security is weakened. There is a strong feeling that America must be number one; we cannot be content with parity.

I suppose there is a sense in which no nation completely trusts another. All nations act in what they believe to be self-interest. In a sinful world, the justification for arms reduction is that our systems of inspection have become so sophisticated that if either side cheats, they will be caught. We acknowledge, of course, that a 100 percent foolproof system is impossible. But so is 100 percent security impossible. And every day we are trusting the enemy to possess sufficient restraint not to initiate war. Parity may represent our best chance of maintaining peace. If either side feels the other is superior, in a time of tension the weaker will be tempted to resort to a first strike in an effort to negate the other's superiority.

As Christians we must encourage all efforts to control the arms race, to negotiate, to find mutual ground for maintaining peace. The 1988 General Conference adopted a resolution which said in part:

> Our goal of world disarmament would be achieved through intermediate steps of arms reduction. We reject deterrence as a permanent basis for the securing and maintenance of peace. It can only be tolerated as a temporary expedient and while real measures of disarmament are set in motion. We affirm measures, particularly between the U.S.S.R. and the United States which develop trust in negotiating postures, and deplore words and actions of one or the other of the major nuclear powers designed to threaten the other.[46]

We understand this to be the moral Christian response.

I am not a genuine pacifist. Every community must have a police force to restrain those who are not amenable to law. Being passive and nonresistant in Germany did not save the Jew. I am convinced that unless you are willing to surrender your life, as Jesus did, you cannot be a true pacifist. But this does not preclude every one of us from working for peace. Treaties, arms control talks, cultural exchanges are some of the ways we use to maintain restraint and sanity in a nuclear world. All the rhetoric about being number one is nonsense. When more than one nation has the bomb, there is no number one. Therefore, we must be willing to talk with the enemy, understand the so-called enemy, and conduct ourselves with dignity and religious maturity even when provoked.

Violets Cracking Rocks

In an article I once read about Tennessee Williams, the playwright was described as a lonely and frightened man. His plays present a world of shattered hopes and failed visions. While he loved his characters, they, as did Williams, struggle against the frightening blankness of their lives. But toward the end of Williams' life, said the writer of the article, he was writing about "the power of violets cracking the rocks." What a beautiful bit of imagery for Christians—violets cracking rocks. Jesus spoke of leaven, salt, a mustard seed.

If the "winds of war" are still howling through our world, so are the winds of God. The good news is of God's countervailing wind that offers hope and healing and peace—through persons who care, who pray, who work for peace and are unwilling to surrender the world to the forces of evil. And the statements and resolutions from the Council of Bishops are designed to encourage us as persons of goodwill to *keep* working and praying.

The film *Gandhi,* produced during the Eighties, has many memorable scenes, but one in particular gives instruction to us. A young Hindu from the slums, both a victim and a doer of violence, confronts Gandhi. Seeking vengeance for the death of his own son at Moslem hands, the Hindu has killed a Moslem boy, crushing the child's head against a wall. "I am going to hell," he says to Gandhi. In his tormented face, you see that he is already there.

Gandhi, lying on a cot and nearly dead from the fast he began to protest the riots, looks at the man and says, "I know a way out of hell. Find a child whose parents have been killed in the riots; adopt and love the child as your own. But let it be a Moslem orphan and raise the child as a Moslem." The haggard man kneels by the cot and rests his head on Gandhi's knees. That is the way of forgiveness, of peace, of self-giving. And Christians are called to offer that kind of example to the world.

Recently I saw a picture of Mother Teresa. Her nose looms large and flat. Her cheeks are deep-caved with advancing age and unrelenting work. Puckers ring her time-worn mouth. Creases chisel their meandering course across her features. It is one of the best-known, best-loved, most-admired faces on earth. Mere worldly beauty cannot match it. "There are no shadows about her," someone once said. Called "The Saint of the Gutters," she travels from Calcutta to Kenya, from Haiti to Hong Kong, from Chicago to Sri Lanka to found relief centers. And hospitals. And orphanages. And "homes of the dying destitute" like the one in India where her merciful work began in 1952. The basic belief animating her life is simple enough: Every person was born to love and to be loved— simple but not easy.

This gnome of a woman has been honored by princes, presidents, and the Pope. She has won the Jewel of India, the Medal of Freedom, and the Nobel Prize for Peace. She is a "violet cracking rocks." I disagree with some of her positions. As indicated earlier in this book, she can be strident and uncompromising when opposing abortion. But she also has demonstrated the difference one person can make in this world.

While talking with a commander in Japan about the Bishops' pastoral letter, "In Defense of Creation," he said, "I don't think church leaders should get involved in matters of foreign policy and peace. That's the job of the military and our political leaders." I said in response, "If you can assure that only politicians and military people will be involved if another war comes, then perhaps what you say is appropriate. But since that is not true, then working for peace is the responsibility of everyone." God, through Christ, calls each of us to be a peacemaker, guided by eternal truth.

12

Boycotts and Civil Disobedience

Few actions of the General Conference of The United Methodist Church are more subject to misunderstanding than the endorsement of boycotts. The General Conference has, at various times, recommended boycotting the Royal Dutch/Shell Company and the Nestlé Company, while the General Board of Church and Society voted in 1988 to continue its participation in the hotly disputed boycott of most California table grapes. Why these actions?

Church and Society voted a boycott of California table grapes in an effort to support the attempt of California farmworkers to establish collective bargaining rights. A boycott of Shell products was recommended because of Royal Dutch/Shell's special contribution to the apartheid system through sales of oil to the South African military and police. The Nestlé boycott was designed to pressure the company into discontinuing the distribution of its infant formula in developing nations. Many are convinced that the promotion and distribution of infant formula contributes nutritional harm to infants in areas of chronic poverty, illiteracy, and inadequate hygienic conditions.

The use of boycotts as a strategy for bringing about social change is not limited to The United Methodist Church. There are organizations that urge the boycotting of the products of companies that sponsor pornographic movies and television programs. Every day, as I drive to my office at the church, I see protesters in front of a medical facility which performs abortions. Boycotts and protest movements do become a way of gaining public attention and effecting social change.

The 1984 General Conference, recognizing that boycotts have validity but may also be subject to abuse, adopted the following resolution:

Whereas, economic boycott of the products of companies engaged in unethical and socially irresponsible practices has sometimes proved to be an effective means of influencing reconsideration and change of such practices; and Whereas, economic boycott is an ethically and legally permissible means of seeking such reform under some circumstances; and Whereas, church bodies as well as individual Christians have sometimes joined in sponsorship of economic boycott; and . . . Whereas, the church is in need of a clear review of the criteria justifying the use of boycott methods as well as other factors pertinent to consideration of economic boycott; *Therefore Be It Resolved,* that the 1984 General Conference: Urge all United Methodist and organizational units of the church, when considering participation in economic boycotts, to study the circumstances carefully in order to determine whether such coercive methods are truly necessary and whether it will be possible to undertake them responsibly and in harmony with the Christian faith.[47]

Infant Formula

The United Methodist Church, in its early boycott of the Nestlé Company products, was joining many other denominations and secular organizations in expressing concern for infant nutrition in developing countries. After a number of years of boycott, protest, and agitation on the part of many different churches and organizations, a "peace treaty" was signed. In January of 1984, representatives of the International Nestlé Boycott Committee and the executive vice president of Nestlé signed a joint statement to the effect that INBC (International Nestlé Boycott Commitee) commended Nestlé for taking the leadership role in compliance with the International Code of the World Health Organization. Nestlé in turn recognized and supported the commitment of INBC and its members to safeguard the children of the Third World from hazards related to the inappropriate marketing of infant formula. The director of the Interfaith Center on Corporate Responsibility, which had served as a base for the boycott, said it marked "one of the most exciting corporate responsibility achievements in the past decade."

This is one example where a boycott was effective. The giant Swiss-based corporation, Nestlé, was the largest producer of infant formula. In an effort to expand its market, it would make free samples available to new mothers in Third World countries, and after they had used this for a few days they would not then be able to breastfeed their babies. This made them dependent upon the formula. But they had neither the money nor the pure water necessary to use the commercial product.

A few concerned persons, aware of this problem, began demanding that changes be made in the well-established and highly successful sales technique. The boycotters were convinced that Nestlé was putting sales ahead of the health of children. In July 1977, when the boycott was first instituted, Nestlé did not take it seriously. The company did not realize to what extent a determined group in the United States could grab the press. Apparently Nestlé never was greatly worried about the boycott's immediate financial effects; its profits rose from $349 million in 1977 to $540 million in 1982.

But the image question did make inroads. It became a drain on management time and on their nerves. The struggle had effects on company morale. Some employees began to wonder if some of the accusations might be true. And undoubtedly the company management, genuinely wanting to be ethical as well as make money, began to consider the validity of the complaints. Trust emerged when company leaders began to understand what it meant for the churches to be involved, and the church leaders became more trusting when they realized the company management was serious about their responsibilities to their Third World constituencies. They gave up media advertising in developing nations, no longer sent out sales representatives dressed like nurses, discontinued giving expensive gifts to doctors and health workers, and stopped the practice of giving "discharge packs" to mothers leaving hospitals or birthing clinics.

In the opinion of many people, it was and is a remarkable story. A director of UNICEF said that lives of more than 1 million children could be saved every year by applying the WHO Infant Formula Code, making changes in medical and hospital practices, promoting breastfeeding, and encouraging safe weaning practices. It is obvious that the boycott activities of the churches and the many other groups and individuals helped bring worldwide attention to the possibility of saving babies' lives. And the Nestlé Corporation gained something of a reputation for being a leader in looking not just at profits but at the social dimensions of its activities.

Apartheid in South Africa

The effectiveness of boycotts in bringing about social change in South Africa is less certain. A majority of the annual conferences of The United Methodist Church have urged the General Board of Pensions of the denomination to sell their stock in companies that do business in South Africa. This is called "divestment." Furthermore, the 1988 General Conference voted a boycott of Shell products, although this was suspended until the Judicial Council could rule on its constitutionality according to church law. But the intent of the Conference was clear, even though the vote was close.

The United States government, the trustees of many universities, and the legislative bodies of nearly all the mainline denominations, have taken positions opposing the practice of apartheid. The General Council of the World Alliance of Reformed Churches (the dominant church in South Africa is a member of this Alliance), in a resolution adopted in 1982 said that apartheid was a sin and could in no way be justified morally or theologically. Most denominations have made similar statements.

The United States House of Representatives has considered and passed various bills that impose sanctions on South Africa, all in an effort to bring changes through economic pressure. South African leaders Archbishop Desmond Tutu and the Reverend Alan Boesak, along with many others, have consistently called for stronger sanctions against the apartheid government. They believe comprehensive sanctions globally applied will maximize pressure on the Pretoria regime, sending a clear message that the international community will no longer tolerate the government's continued acts of violence toward anti-apartheid groups.

The reason the General Conference called for the Shell boycott is that South Africa is a nation without its own supply of oil. Royal Dutch/Shell co-owns or operates oil refinery facilities in South Africa. The oil refined by Shell in South Africa supplies government agencies, including the police and military, which are used to maintain apartheid. For years, British, Dutch, and U.S. churches have been in dialogue with Shell. The 1984 United Methodist General Conference in the resolution "South Africa" specifically urged "divestment from corporations doing business in South Africa; an end to any collaboration with South Africa by opposing expanded participation of corporations in the South Africa economy; and support of United Nations' sanctions against South Africa."

The 1988 resolution says:

> The United Methodist Church joins the boycott of Royal Dutch/Shell and asks that its units and members refrain from purchasing Shell products so long as the boycott continues. Participation in the boycott will end when Royal Dutch/Shell withdraws from South Africa and terminates all license and franchise agreements with South African entities or when the apartheid system ceases.[48]

The intent of the boycott, obviously, is to increase pressure on the South African government to end its policies which legally separate the races.

Shell's press representative in New York, upon being informed of the proposed boycott, said Shell Oil was disappointed and surprised at the call for a boycott. He said that the boycott was not fair particularly for Shell service station dealers, almost all of whom are independent business people. He also said that people grossly misrepresent the actions and views of the company, which condemns apartheid as being inhuman and believes apartheid should be abolished quickly and peacefully.

The representative of the company also indicated that the policy of their organization was to work within the system and from that position endeavor to effect changes in the immoral practice of apartheid. This raises an interesting question. Do you try to bring about changes from a posture of working within the system or stand apart from it and attempt to impose external pressure that finally causes the government of South Africa to surrender its long-held position?

Some people question the effectiveness of boycotts when dealing with a national government. For example, they might point out that as American businesses have left South Africa, they have taken their anti-apartheid programs with them. During the decade of the Eighties, U.S. corporations in South Africa spent more than $210 million on education, training, and housing of their black employees and their families, on health facilities, and on legal aid. Withdrawal of these firms has inevitably meant reduction of these programs, to the detriment of future black leadership and its participation in the post-apartheid era. Once gone, the influence such firms exercised on the local scene is also gone. Furthermore, these companies are usually sold either to South Africans at bargain rates or to other foreign investors who do not have the same commitment to eradicating apatheid that some U.S. companies manifested. Most of the new owners do not subscribe to the Sullivan Principles that were designed to undermine apartheid.

One researcher reports that the departure of Western capital may hurt South Africa in the long run—but that for now, nearly all the once-American plants continue to operate profitably under new ownership. Western sanctions have meant windfall profits for the South African investors who have bought their assets at fire-sale prices. But some South Africans have been hurt. For instance, black fishermen can no longer sell their lobsters for export to the United States, which used to buy $30 million worth a year. The coal, mined by black coal miners, can no longer be sold to the American market. An estimated 10,000 of them were fired after sanctions were imposed by our Congress. When trade and investment are discouraged in South Africa, that undermines the surest mechanism for the peaceful expansion of black rights and power, which is an expanding economy. Since the release of Nelson Mandela from prison, the South African government has made major changes in its apartheid laws. It is difficult to assess the role of boycotts in hastening these shifts in policy, but it is apparent that they have played a role.

All of this suggests, however, that there are no easy solutions. Boycotts apparently do have some value when the target is a single corporation which has a sense of ethical responsibility such as the Nestlé Company. The value and effect are not so clear when the effort is to change the policies of a government. This is one of the reasons the 1984 General Conference passed the resolution mentioned earlier, urging all United Methodists, "when considering participation in economic boycotts, to study the circumstances carefully in order to determine whether such coercive methods are truly necessary and whether it will be possible to undertake them responsibly and in harmony with the Christian faith."

Those of us who have enjoyed a leadership role in the denomination should examine one implication of our endorsement of boycotts. Is the General Conference, by using this procedure, training the local church to use the same process when trying to effect some change in the denomination? The United Methodist Church is a member of the World Council of Churches. I approve this. No one of us necessarily endorses all the statements issued by the Council, but as E. Stanley Jones once said, "Everyone who names the name of Christ should be in conversation with all others who name his name." And as Wesley reminded his followers, "We are people of catholic spirit." We belong to each other.

When someone suggests to me that we should get out of the World Council of Churches, I usually ask: "Where do you want us to go? Do you want us to stand in a corner by ourselves?" But through the years I have found many parishioners unhappy with the denomination's membership in the World Council. Some of them have written letters threatening to withhold their pledge until some change is made. Some pastors and district superintendents become very upset when this happens. My response is: "But we trained them to do that when we approved boycotts as a way of accomplishing systemic changes. Why blame the laity if they do at the local level what we do at the national level?" I know there are differences, but I also believe that the laity have the same right to practice boycotts at the local level when attempting to bring about some modification in the denomination as the General Church has when attempting to accomplish some desired change in society.

Civil Disobedience

Governments and laws should be servants of God and of human beings. Citizens have a duty to abide by laws duly adopted by orderly and just process of government. But governments, no less than individuals, are subject to the judgment of God. Therefore, we recognize the right of individuals to dissent when acting under the constraint of conscience and after exhausting all legal recourse, to disobey laws deemed to be unjust. Even then, respect for law should be shown by refraining from violence and by accepting the costs of disobedience.[49]

Civil disobedience is different from a boycott, yet it is similar. It is simply a more aggressive way of protesting. The most obvious form civil disobedience now takes is the fight against abortion by pro-life activists. Antiabortion sit-ins have resulted in thousands of arrests and hundreds of persons jailed.

A. J. Muste, a leading figure in resistance to America's wars from World War I to Vietnam, writes:

Nonconformity, Holy Disobedience, becomes a virtue, indeed a necessary and indispensable measure of spiritual self-preservation, in a day when the impulse to conform, to acquiesce, to go along, is used as an instrument to subject men to totalitarian rule and involve them in permanent war. . . . The church could lead the way in a disciplined and prayerful movement of nonviolent action. An approach to civil disobedience that is biblically, pastorally, and politically sound is greatly needed at the local church level.[50]

Some members of the United Church of Christ were arrested when they entered the Capitol rotunda in Washington, DC to protest our national policy in Central America. Some parishioners in that denomination claimed this was "left-wing activism" and blamed civil disobedience for everything from declining church membership to the breakup of traditional American family life. During the civil rights controversy of the Sixties, those who violated the segregation laws were called "left-wing." Those who now break the trespass laws in protesting abortion are labeled "right-wing." Perhaps labels are more in the eye of the beholder than anywhere else. But the question we raise concerns the appropriateness and morality of civil disobedience.

Civil disobedience is not new to the church. Throughout time, people of God have faced moments of truth in which they have had to decide either to obey human edicts or respond to more compelling laws written on their hearts. Biblical heroine Esther declared, "If I perish, I perish," then went to see the king, illegally, thereby saving her people from annihilation (Esther 4:16). Likewise, Daniel and the three Hebrews, the apostles and scores of first century Christians faced lions, fires, and torture rather than obey ungodly laws.

By nature, civil disobedience creates tension. Martin Luther King, Jr. responded to this feeling in his "Letter from Birmingham Jail," after being denounced by fellow clergy for leading "unwise and untimely" sit-ins at segregated Alabama lunch counters:

> You deplore the demonstrations that are presently taking place in Birmingham. But I am sorry that your statement did not express a similar concern for the conditions that brought the demonstrations into being. . . .
>
> You are exactly right in your call for negotiation. Indeed, this is the purpose of direct action. Nonviolent direct action seeks to create such a crisis and establish such creative tension that a community that has constantly refused to negotiate is forced to confront the issue.[51]

Political activism in the United States is as old as our nation. We remember with great pride the fact that angry colonists dressed as Indians dumped British tea in the Boston harbor as a protest against British taxation. Yet there is much reason to respect law. Even the frequently imprisoned Apostle Paul had high regard for civil law and urged Christians to be law-abiding citizens under the rule of imperial Rome, pagan and oppressive though it was. In Romans 13 he wrote:

> Let every person be subject to the governing authorities; for there is no authority except from God, and those authorities that exist have been instituted by God. Therefore whoever resists authority resists what God has appointed, and those who resist will incur judgment. For rulers are not a terror to good conduct, but to bad. Do you wish to have no fear of the authority? Then do what is good, and you will receive its approval; for it is God's servant for your good (1-4).

I know there are occasions when it seems there is no recourse except to violate some law in order to test its constitutionality. There are times when a person must take a stand and also accept the consequences. A news article told of forty prominent Americans who were jailed for protesting South Africa's apartheid policies. One of them said, "Ours was an act of conscience in response to the repressive action of the South African government with respect to the noble, nonviolent protest of black South Africans over the last few months." One member of Congress who is also a Baptist pastor called his arrest and night in jail "an act of moral witness." Gandhi once said that "non-cooperation with evil is as much a duty as cooperation with good." Civil disobedience is especially powerful when it can serve as a catalyst for other acts of non-cooperation with evil, where its example of moral freedom is so clear and contagious that it can ignite the spirit of a larger community. This was what happened during the days of the civil rights protest, and it is what those interested in changing current abortion practice hope will happen.

In April 1963, Martin Luther King, Jr. was imprisoned for eight days as a result of his role in the Birmingham, Alabama, civil rights campaign. During that time, as indicated earlier, he wrote the famous "Letter from Birmingham Jail." He also wrote:

> I hope you can see the distinction I am trying to point out. In no sense do I advocate evading or defying the law as the rabid segregationist would do. This would lead to anarchy. One who breaks an unjust law must do it openly, lovingly . . . and with a willingness to accept the penalty. I submit that an individual who breaks a law that conscience tells him is unjust, and willingly accepts the penalty by staying in jail to arouse the conscience of the community over its injustice, is in reality expressing the very highest respect for law.[52]

I suppose what King was saying is easier to evaluate in the context of a Christian in Holland or Germany choosing to defy the law and hide a Jew during the holocaust—or a Christian in China defying the Cultural Revolution and inviting friends to a service of worship in the home. But it is also true that our unjust segregation laws in the United States had to be challenged and changed. When Rosa Parks refused to go to the back of the bus, or give her seat to a white, after she had been working all day, she was making a moral witness.

At the same time, there are many reasons for respecting the law, and violations should be made only for the most serious of reasons. In this country most adults have had opportunity, whether used or not, to participate in the process of making laws and choosing those who enforce them. We are not living under a foreign power. We have chosen our leaders. And most of us depend upon and profit by some services of government.

In *Responsible Freedom*, L. Harold DeWolf points out:

> The alternative to law-abiding order must also be considered. If this were to be broken down generally, business and transportation would be quickly disrupted. In the cities where most of our people live, food would soon become unavailable. In a common scramble for life's necessities, the strong and ruthless would plunder and destroy, while the weak and helpless would be trampled under foot. Widespread civil disturbance would be far more destructive than in former years, because elaborate industrialization and dense population have established such a delicate fabric of complex interdependence. To take part in breaking down respect for law is an exceedingly serious act.[53]

De Wolf, who taught at one of the United Methodist seminaries, says there are three reasons why someone may feel it necessary to engage in civil disobedience: 1) testing and overthrowing invalid laws; 2) in forced dilemmas of conscience; (The apostle Peter said: "We must obey God rather than men." If the state commands what the citizen is convinced God forbids, the Christian must follow conscience. After World War II the United States actively supported a movement in the United Nations to bring to trial various German Nazis for acts of crime "under international law." The International Law Commission established for the purpose formulated principles to govern the Nuremberg Tribunal in the trials. One is especially relevant to this discussion. It says: "The fact that a person acted pursuant to order of his Government or a superior does not relieve him from responsibility under international law, provided a moral choice was in fact possible to him." Under this provision many men were, in fact, judged guilty and hanged or sentenced to imprisonment.) 3) as a means of revolutionary change. (We remember that our nation gained independence through revolution against the English crown. Leading up to the actual war were acts of deliberate refusal to pay taxes, to obey British officials, and to acknowledge the authority of laws made in London.)

But always, for the Christian, there must be compelling reasons if the path of dissent is chosen. The risks are great. If the social fabric of the nation is torn too frequently, who can be protected? All will suffer. There was a time in this nation when the legal system did great violence to minorities and the poor. Such violence justified radical protest and drastic means of change. But even then, care was exercised in redressing the wrong so there was minimum damage to people—especially those suffering the most. I think we can conclude that some small-scale civil disobedience deliberately designed to focus attention and stir action may be useful in some places and times, but always there must be the search for practical, effective channels that can also create change without threatening the duly established legal options that must finally assure security and tranquility for all citizens.

Sanctuary

On one occasion I was asked to participate in a special service in a church in Minneapolis that was declaring itself to be a sanctuary for illegal aliens. A number of congregations, in a variety of denominations, took this action and harbored refugees from Central America who, if sent home, might be killed by their own government. Sanctuary is a powerful symbol of the limits of the authority of the state. Under medieval English law, a fugitive in an officially recognized sanctuary could "abjure the realm" and move from the sanctuary out of the country in safety. The sanctuary represented an order which transcended the sovereignty of the nation-state.

The 1984 General Conference adopted the following resolution:

> Whereas, at various times in history the Christian Church has been called upon to give concrete evidence of its commitment to love and justice even when it seems contrary to public opinion; and Whereas, according to the terms of the Refugee Act of 1980 the United States accords refugee or asylum status to persons who cannot return to their countries of origin because of persecution or fear of persecution, for reasons of race, religion, nationality, membership in a particular social group or political opinion; and Whereas, refugees from Central America and other areas of Latin America and the Caribbean are fleeing to the United States to escape the persecution, torture, and murder of their civil-war-torn homelands; and Whereas, many of these refugees have been tortured and murdered when forced to return to their homelands; and Whereas, Scripture says not to mistreat foreigners who live in your land (Lev. 19:33) because sojourners and strangers have a special place in the heart of God. THEREFORE, BE IT RESOLVED, that The United Methodist Church strongly: Urges the President of the United States . . . to grant "extended voluntary departure" legal status to refugees . . . (and) Encourages congregations who take seriously the mandate to do justice and to resist the policy of the Immigration and Naturalization Service by declaring their churches to be "sanctuaries" for refugees. . . . [54]

What should be our attitude toward sheltering illegal aliens from Central America, thus risking a serious confrontation between church and state? Is this a function for a church? The government claims most of the Central American aliens are not running from death squads but are pursuing jobs. And some who oppose the sanctuary movement say it is not primarily a humanitarian response to persons in jeopardy of their lives but an organized protest against American policy in Central America. Sanctuary as a humanitarian concern is one thing but sanctuary as opposition to American policy in Central America is quite another. Concerned Christians who want to respond responsibly to the sanctuary issue should look carefully at both sides of the debate and grapple with both sets of scripture—those concerning refugees and displaced persons as well as those dealing with obedience to government.

In 1968 I was serving as a pastor in Cincinnati. I was also a delegate to the General Conference of that year which met in Dallas. One action of the Conference was a resolution supporting the right of minority groups to violate segregation laws and test their constitutionality. Condemning children to live in rat-infested tenements, to be permanently handicapped physically and mentally by a low-protein diet, to have self-respect crushed by racist attitudes, and even to be bullied by prejudiced police who were acting in accordance with immoral segregation laws was intolerable to Christian conscience.

The Conference said persons humiliated by such laws had a right to disobey them and seek redress. Following the action of the Conference, this headline appeared in a Cincinnati newspaper: "Methodists Endorse Right to Disobey Law." In the spring of 1967, following the assassination of Martin Luther King, Jr., there had been racial riots in a number of our cities, including Cincinnati. In this context of tension and fear, the newspaper headline was inflammatory and caused much uneasiness. As a pastor, I received a large number of protest letters from parishioners. I remember one woman who wrote and asked that her church membership be discontinued. I visited in her home, and in the course of our conversation, she took me into a room that was decorated and furnished almost as a meditation center. The lights were subdued. There was an American flag and a Confederate flag. Hanging on the wall were framed letters written by a great-grandfather who was a soldier in the War between the States. There was a lighted candle. I stood there for a moment, waiting for her to speak. Then she said: "I wanted you to see this so you would know how important my country is to me. You have forced me to choose between my country and my church, and I choose my country. That is why I am dropping my membership."

I was saddened as I left. In a way, I understood. Her world, formerly secure and predictable, was changing more rapidly than she could accept. The General Conference action seemed very threatening. I was sorry she felt she had to choose between her church and her country. Most of us would feel that there are times when to be a loving critic is the highest form of patriotism. We are expected, in a democracy, to resist and struggle against whatever we see that we believe to be, from the Christian perspective, evil and unjust. In such situations, we must respond with protest and noncooperation. In the judgment of the General Conference, segregation laws were inherently immoral and were to be challenged. But my parishioner saw this as an expression of disloyalty which would ultimately disrupt the orderly processes of our community. After the emotions of that turbulent era in our national life subsided, she and her husband returned to the church as frequent participants in worship, although she never asked that her membership be restored.

Protests and civil disobedience should be measures of last resort. The Bible encourages us, "Come, let us reason together." At its best, law is designed to enhance the effective functioning of the community and safeguard the peace, tranquility, and well-being of all citizens.

Wide and judicious use of protest and civil disobedience is very much a part of the Christian heritage and an honored part of our national history. Early Christian leaders would be considered pacifists. But they were far from passive in their response to persecution. They poured forth a torrent of protest, defiance, and censure against the persecutors and their decrees. However, unlike those who chose a military response to oppression, they acted without violence and with a willingness to endure suffering for their faith.

We are people of conscience. We are people of conviction. We are people who want the highest good for all persons. We want to accomplish our goals through kindness, peaceably, but with firmness and resolution. But we also live by the words and example of Martin Luther who said to the established powers of the sixteenth century: "Here I stand; I cannot do otherwise."

13

Church vs. State

Recent presidential campaigns have made the American people increasingly aware of issues that involve church-state relationships, particularly such matters as prayer in public schools. The Social Principles deal with this in a number of ways. An introductory statement says: "While our allegiance to God takes precedence over our allegiance to any state, we acknowledge the vital function of government as a principal vehicle for the ordering of society." Traditional wisdom holds that one way to keep friends is to avoid conversations about religion and politics. More and more, however, the two topics, often intertwined, are forcing their way onto the front pages and evening news reports.

The founders of this nation presented the concept of separation of church and state. Ever since, it has been in a constant state of interpretation and refinement as attempts have been made to accommodate the concept to specific historical circumstances. The present time is a crucial period of debate and searching. There are many controversial issues in addition to prayer in public schools, such as government chaplaincies, tax exemption for churches, and church participation in public affairs. The intent of this chapter is to examine some of these concerns from the perspective of the Social Principles of The United Methodist Church.

Emotions are not as high now as they were in 1960 during the candidacy of John F. Kennedy for the presidency. One survey indicated that more than 25 percent of the people said they could not vote for him because they feared he would, as a Roman Catholic, violate the historic principle of separation of church and state. More recent surveys indicate that only about 8 percent of the people would be influenced by denominational bias when voting for a candidate. But there are many issues before the nation that generate considerable passion and become divisive. Church/state issues have always been and continue to be of great importance to the American people.

Politics and Religion

Politics has been defined as a community's struggle over how to act—a struggle which has immense consequences in human lives. Christians, and, in our case, United Methodists, cannot stand aloof from it. Noted public affairs commentator Bill Moyers has said that religion is perhaps the most determinative force in shaping a social vision. While we heartily endorse separation of church and state, we also recognize that they are intertwined.

After speaking at a local church, in a follow-up discussion I asked what came to mind when I said "annual conference." The first person to speak said, "Politics." A few weeks later, in a similar situation at another church, I posed the same question and received the same answer: "Politics."

Politics carries a negative connotation but is an honorable word. In a country with a dictator, there is little politics. One person, or a small clique, makes the decisions. In religions that practice mind control, there is little by way of politics. A few people do the thinking and the rest must follow. Politics is the expression of opinions, the effort to persuade others to a point of view. It is taking a vote and accepting the decision made in a democratic way. This is the way a denomination such as ours does its work. There is debate. There is compromise. At times one person will lose, on another occasion win. But through it all, there is the Body of Christ at work, trying to find the will of the Spirit and making appropriate and helpful decisions.

In similar fashion, politics is the nation at work, sorting out the direction it wishes to take. The democratic process, with debate, persuasion, and vote may not be too efficient, but I don't know of any other process that would be better. And the church has a place in this, expressing its point of view, trying to persuade others, but then bowing to the will of the majority. The Social Principles of our church say:

> We believe that the state should not attempt to control the Church, nor should the Church seek to dominate the state. "Separation of church and state" means no organic union of the two, but does permit interaction. The Church should continually exert a strong ethical influence upon the state, supporting policies and programs deemed to be just and compassionate and opposing policies and programs which are not.[55]

In other words, United Methodists believe we must be involved in the political process, making our opinions known but never trying

How many have ever written letters / PC/ called re: a political issue to control the state even as we resist any effort of the state to control the church as has so often been true in fascist and communist countries.

When any segment of the church becomes too identified with a particular party, it is then viewed by the politicians as one more constituency to be exploited. Every religious group should express its position. But to become involved in partisan politics by endorsing candidates is of dubious value both to the church and to the political process.

A brief review of history helps in understanding this position. During the first 1600 years of church history, the question of separation of church and state aroused little interest because the answer was obvious. In Western civilization, church and state were usually wedded even as they are today in such countries as Iran, Israel, Pakistan, Italy, and numerous others where the link is openly acknowledged. In England, the monarch is still legally the head of the church.

Our own pilgrim forebears assumed the two would be joined. But in time they discovered, as did John Calvin in Geneva, that a church invested with national authority can become oppressive. The witch hunt was the more dramatic form this took in our own history.

Finally, through the efforts of many persons, notably Roger Williams, who played a role in the establishment of Rhode Island, the idea of the separation of church and state was accepted. Historians call this the "Great Experiment."

By the time of the writing of the Constitution, the pluralistic character of our society was apparent. The First Amendment to the Constitution guarantees that Congress shall make no law respecting the establishment of religion. It must be emphasized that this was not intended to be anti-religion. It simply means the state shall not dominate the church nor the church the state.

Nor does it prevent the national government from being concerned about the church. Churches do not pay taxes on the buildings used for worship, and clergy are exempt from the selective service. Furthermore, as already indicated, the church is not prevented from making its point of view known. The First Amendment to the Constitution also supports the right of citizens to "petition the government for redress of grievances." If the church officially becomes a lobby, however, it can lose its tax-exempt status.

Aristotle defined politics as the art of making and keeping people truly human. Therefore, the gospel must have something to say about the way we spend our tax dollars. Do they enhance life or dehumanize? Most social, economic, and political issues have religious implications. By way of historic precedent for United Methodists, John Wesley once said, "We have nothing to do but save souls." But he also said, "I have no religion but a social religion." And the revival of which he was a part in eighteenth-century England made a unique contribution to the abolition of the slave trade, prison reform, and the birth and development of a political party which gave workers a voice.

When Hitler came to power, many people assumed that the universities or the press would speak out against the atrocities. However, these forces were silenced. Only the church could stand across the path of Hitler's campaign.

Of course, not all the churches in Germany refused to bow the knee to Baal. There were some—Niemoller, Bonhoeffer, and others of less fame—who went to jail or concentration camps while proclaiming that even the state was under the judgment of God. There are occasional moments when the church must rise up and say to the state that its goals must be reexamined in the uncomfortable glare of biblical morality, that its leaders are to be judged by eternal standards. The church may not know how to offer political and military advice, but it can and must, on occasion, express moral outrage. It has an obligation to convey its concerns.

But church leaders must realize that decisions concerning economics, politics, and diplomacy have to be made ultimately by persons who actually bear the consequences of their decisions. Those who serve the nation in other ways certainly have the right and obligation to be critical, to challenge, to oppose some policies and to encourage others. Ultimately, however, it is those who have the power and the responsibility who must make the decisions, shape the policy, and determine the action. The church and its leaders must temper any inclination to arrogance and self-assurance by the awareness that those who actually carry the burden of decision are the ones who have to shape policy.

We live in a democratic, pluralistic society. Persons of equal commitment and wisdom disagree vigorously with respect to specific issues. We must, therefore, not say, "Thus saith the Lord." We can surely say, "This is the way I see it. This is my best judgment." But we do that knowing there are others, equally honest, equally able, who are committed to quite an opposite view. It is in the ferment of competing ideas that truth may emerge. This is why the church and its leaders have a vital part in the ongoing dialogue. Pluralism means there will be a variety of perspectives within a given community. Decisions on public policy in such a society are not dictated by religious authority but determined through a democratic process, and the church participates as one among many voices. But speak it must!

Not a Christian Nation

Religious freedom is a characteristic of this nation which most United Methodists affirm. This means the state will not require us to affirm beliefs we do not hold or to engage in acts of worship that do not conform to our inner state of mind.

Religious liberty also means the freedom to communicate our convictions to others. There are countries where it is against the law to endeavor to persuade another person to your religious point of view. This is true in many Moslem countries. Christians are not permitted to proselytize Jews in Israel. Furthermore, religious freedom means the freedom to act on the basis of one's religious convictions. Such religious liberty includes the right to be a Christian, a Moslem, a Mormon, an agnostic, an atheist—to choose to believe or even to choose to deny God. Bishop Leroy Hodapp in a 1985 address said:

> Based upon this principle, the United States is not—and never has been—a Christian nation; any more than we are a Buddhist nation, or a Jewish nation, or a Mormon nation, or an atheistic nation, or a secular nation. We are a nation in which persons freely may profess any given religious faith or no religious faith—and still be as qualified and acceptable a United States citizen as any other. This freedom has provided a fertile ground in which the Christian faith has grown to become the dominant faith in the nation—but as the largest it has no more right to support or protection by the state than the smallest religious minority.

Interestingly, in late 1988 the Arizona Republican State Convention passed a resolution declaring the United States to be under the rule of Jesus Christ and declared the United States to be a "Christian nation" governed by the "absolute laws" of scripture. This action provided a problem for the Christians present who interpret the scriptures variously, but also for the party's chairman, who was Jewish. On the side of the vote was former Governor Evan Mecham who said, "The United States is a Christian nation, and I don't care who doesn't like it," but the gray eminence of the party, Senator Barry Goldwater, a Christian of Jewish origins, dismissed the resolution as the work of "kooks." The chairman responded to the resolution by proposing a new one for the party's executive committee to consider that would declare the party "open to all faiths, all peoples, and all races." The confusion that resulted from the action of the state convention illustrates the difficulties that result from any attempt to declare this to be a "Christian nation."

Basically, Americans and United Methodists want freedom of religion and a mood of tolerance. Recent polls indicate we are more accepting of religious differences than we were a few years ago. But our tolerance is tempered by wariness: 21 percent of us wouldn't vote for a pastor for president; 51 percent of us favor a high wall of separation between church and state; and 57 percent of us don't want organized religious groups meddling in politics. In fact, a slight plurality of us—45 percent to 44 percent—think some religious groups threaten our democracy. Suspicion of organized religion has deep roots. Many of our forebears came here to escape religious persecution. They didn't want a state church standing between them and God or telling them what to believe. That is why, in spite of the fact that the majority religion in this country is Christian, we are still not a "Christian nation."

Sensitivity to this understanding has brought changes in some of our traditions. Government-sponsored nativity and menorah displays—once a standard mix of the secular and the sacred—are under attack by forces advocating the strict separation of church and state.

In 1984, The Supreme Court allowed communities to include nativity scenes and other religious symbols in holiday displays sponsored by governments if the religious symbols were part of displays that included Santa Claus, snowmen, and reindeer. This gave the display a "secular" purpose, the court said. But that did not satisfy members of the religious community who were uncomfortable with the idea that the traditional symbols were just part of a secular display. I believe this is a misuse of sacred symbols and subjects them to identification with political interests.

Whether public schools should allow students to participate in religious activities or to sing Christmas carols on school grounds also has been a source of controversy. In Florida, for example, parents of students at one elementary school quarreled for two months over whether the children should be allowed to sing Christmas carols and Hanukkah songs at school functions. No, said a parent-teacher committee formed after some parents, Jewish and Christian, complained that their children felt uncomfortable with the events. Other parents said they wanted their children to sing the songs. After debate and threats of a lawsuit by some parents, school officials agreed to allow only those songs contained in a state-approved textbook.

The United Methodist Church opposes the use of tax funds in a manner which offends any religious group. This means that if there were objection, then we would not encourage displays on public property of nativity scenes nor would we want the school to use songs that are specifically Christian in content. At the same time, we recognize that there are musical classics that though Christian in origin have become the heritage of all persons.

United Methodists believe churches and religious groups are not strengthened by encouraging or permitting the state to assume their rightful role in teaching the faith. As someone has reminded us, the role of the state is to maintain the freedom of all religious bodies to evangelize in the name of their particular faith—but not to involve government in any converting effort.

Following this idea of separation, there are those who advocate the removal of the American flag from the sanctuary of our churches. In my years as a local pastor, we always had the American flag along with the Christian. On the other hand, a pastor in the conference where I served as bishop refused to allow the American flag to be displayed in the church. This was the source of much debate in his community. There are, in my judgment, sound theological reasons for both positions. The church is where we worship God. "Thou shalt have no other gods before me." On the other hand, we do express our identity not only as Christians but as part of a community and nation, and there should be no conflict between the two loyalties. Although, as history reminds us, it can happen. In that I was never troubled personally by the presence of the flag, and "love of God and country" is a basic emotion in our well-being, it does not seem this is an issue of great importance. A professor at one of the seminaries has said: "A wall may separate church and state, but God looks over the wall, reigns over both, overrules the confusion in both, impresses both into service in different ways. In its dealing with the state, as in its own life and work, the church owes absolute obedience to its Lord." Both flags may be appropriate, as long as we never forget to whom we owe our ultimate allegiance.

Prayer in School

There is a saying that as long as there are tests, there will be prayer in the classroom. But it cannot be sponsored by the state. That is the ruling of the Supreme Court. Twice in the Eighties the Court said that even a mandated minute of silence for meditation or voluntary prayer is unconstitutional. It also said that daily moments of silence "for quiet and private contemplation and introspection" violated separation of church and state. In 1962 the Court ruled that government could not advance religion, inhibit religion, or favor one religion over another. Forcing children to pray aloud in school, the court said, clearly violates those principles. Cajoling them to pray in silence is, the court said, a form of "enforced orthodoxy." From the point of view of the court, any kind of organized prayer in public schools, no matter how silent or "voluntary," threatens religious liberty. The court's position is clear: children's religious practices are personal; government should not interfere.

Tony Campolo, an evangelical who has written *Hot Potatoes Christians Are Afraid to Touch*, tells of his personal experience in a public school with Bible reading and prayer. He recalls in a vague way taking part but has concluded it was probably counterproductive. On many occasions, some student would be assigned the task of reading the scriptures so that the teacher could take the roll while the "religious exercises" were going on. The prayer was uttered with anything but reverence. The end result was to trivialize religion.

Those who favor Bible reading and prayer in public schools should remember the consequences this policy might have in parts of the country where Christianity is not the dominant religion. For instance, in Utah, all children would have to sit through the reading of the Book of Mormon. What kind of an impression would this have on them? In Hawaii, where Buddhism is dominant, our youngsters would have to listen to daily readings from the *Baghavad Gita*.

I grew up in a home where we had Bible reading and prayer around the table each morning before going to school. In contemporary society, where frequently both parents are employed and the time for children to depart for school often varies, the model of my youth may no longer work. But families who are serious about the religious instruction of their children will not assume that the school can do it and will personally establish habits and practices that more than compensate for any loss that might have been suffered as a result of the ruling of the Supreme Court regarding religion in public schools. Faith is best fostered in the home and in places consecrated to religion.

There is a concern, of course, that by prohibiting a moment of silence the government may appear hostile toward religion. To counteract that subtle message, United Methodists would encourage social studies and history teachers and textbooks to pay attention to the sweep of religion and religious freedom in the development of this nation. We also affirm the federal equal-access law, which gives student-led religious groups the right to meet on school grounds, and textbooks that include the place of religion in American life. It does not seem right that the role of religion in this country should be ignored in the classroom. Also, during the religious seasons of the year, we do not object to teachers and others saying, "This is a season that Jews, Catholics, Protestants, or Mormons regard as important, and this is why it is significant." This type of education in public schools is appropriate and important.

Teaching Values

A Tennessee judge in 1986 ordered public schools to honor a request by a group of parents that their children be excused from using certain textbooks deemed offensive to their religious convictions. The order stands in a long tradition of court rulings that public education should accommodate religiously based objections often raised by Jewish or Jehovah's Witness parents. In 1987, however, a court in Atlanta reversed the decision. The appeals court found no evidence that omission of references to religion constituted an advancement of secular humanism, as was alleged by the parents. Furthermore, in 1987 the U.S. Supreme Court struck down a Louisiana law that required the teaching of the biblical creation story in public schools whenever evolution is taught. The high court said the law violated the First Amendment because it sought to use government support to achieve a religious purpose.

U.S. News & World Report, in a July 4, 1988, article, expressed concern that while religion has played a crucial role in shaping history, you wouldn't know it from reading today's textbooks. Publishers, in an effort to avoid any possibility of controversy, have dropped mention of religion and moral values from their material. Yet, many argue, you can't have an accurate portrayal of history if you do this, and students, for example, can't really understand the civil rights movement if they don't know that the religious convictions of Martin Luther King, Jr. and other ordained ministers helped give the movement its strong moral fiber. The researchers who wrote the article concluded that public schools may constitutionally teach about religion, if their approach (1) is academic, not devotional; (2) explains the role of religion in history and civilization; (3) takes a literary approach to the study of religious works or aims to make students aware of different religions without implying acceptance of any one religion; (4) does not invoke religious authority to teach moral values; (5) does not promote or denigrate a particular religion.

This is an important development which United Methodists would encourage, particularly if the teachers are well trained in how to fulfill the assignment. But this still does not get at the concern about where youngsters learn values. Can the school assist in this process? The gradual erosion of any reference to religion supposedly leaves a "valueless" education but may in reality teach the religion of "secular humanism." In 1989 the American Jewish Committee endorsed a movement to teach values in public schools, claiming "moral relativism" represents a greater danger than the possibility of church-state abuses. The Committee approved a report by a task force that encourages schools to define and teach values that are at the foundation of a democracy. The National Council of Churches also launched an experimental program to bring together churches, schools, and teacher-education colleges to help communities establish a consensus on values that should be taught.

The Jewish committee's report said that, in many cases, religious and civic values are identical. Among these are compassion, a regard for human worth and dignity, integrity, and justice. The report said a nonsectarian consensus can be reached on what values should be taught. They recognized that there should not be controversy over values such as those listed, but there would be enormous controversy over opening the door for sectarian religion.

Columnist George Cornell, in a survey taken in 1987, said that in a curious inconsistency, most Americans approve the slogan "separation of church and state" but not its results. Most favor public prayers before high school sporting events, a moment of silence in schools for voluntary prayer, and inclusion of biblical perspectives about creation in discussion of evolution. Majorities also say public schools should allow student religious groups to meet in classrooms in off hours and that it's appropriate to put Christian or Jewish holiday symbols on government property. Some of these things the courts have said are not permissible. But it is clear that a majority of the people do want the schools to find some way to be concerned for the whole student, not just the mind and body. A wholistic approach is needed and that includes emotions, convictions, attitudes, values, and the ability to choose between right and wrong.

As I read the results of surveys and study the articles and books that have been written outlining what the American people want, I get excited. There seems to be a growing sense of urgency. I don't think we have given up the dream of what this nation can become for all people. Years ago a football player was talking about the coach who had led the team to the Super Bowl. He said, "He taught us to think like champions." That's what we are trying to do— respect diversity, but teach those values that are essential to fulfill our destiny as a nation.

Government Chaplaincies

The United States Senate and the House of Representatives have chaplains who open their sessions with prayer and are available for counseling and other religious duties. These persons receive compensation from the government. There are chaplains in federal

penitentiaries, veterans' hospitals, and in the various branches of
the military. For six years I served as the chairperson of the committee that endorses United Methodist chaplains. Over four hundred of
our clergy serve in the military and are compensated in the same
way as other members of our defense establishment. On occasion
this system of chaplains paid by the government has been challenged. It does seem to violate the historic separation of church and
state. Yet there is tradition on the side of the present arrangement.
In 1789, the Congress approved the First Amendment to the Constitution and sent it to the states for ratification. Three days later, the
same Congress voted to employ a chaplain. It therefore appears
clear that, from the beginning, governmental chaplaincies were not
seen to be in conflict with the principle of separation of church and
state.

The reason for chaplains seems clear. Persons serving the government, or in prison, and away from home should have the
opportunity to voluntarily practice their religion and should have
the consolation of their faith. While serving on the committee that
endorses chaplains, I went overseas to conduct retreats for military
chaplains and in the process visited a dozen or more of our bases.
Many of those serving in the military are young, in stressful situations, and very much in need of moral and spiritual guidance. The
government feels the responsibility to provide worship services
and offer access to religious nurture. Participation, of course, is
purely voluntary, and chaplains are required to provide the kind of
service the personnel on a given base desires. Chaplains of some
denominations may feel they can only provide worship experiences, sacramental administration, and pastoral care for the ad-
herents of their own faith. United Methodists, however, are noted
for their willingness to meet the needs of every person in their
community to the best of their ability. Increasingly, this means
securing the temporary service of appropriate persons who can
lead an Islamic or Buddhist service, or one addressing the needs of
a particular ethnic community.

The United Methodist Church endorses the concept of chaplains
supported by governmental revenue. Several United Methodist
clergy have served as Chief of Chaplains with the Army, Navy, and
Air Force. We do believe chaplains should only perform duties
related to their primary ministry role. The Division of Chaplains
and Related Ministries of our denomination has instructed our
chaplains not to carry arms under any circumstance. Their role is to
represent the gospel. They are to be the visible presence of the holy
in the midst of the demonic. We also believe that chaplains must
claim the freedom and independence to confront institutions when

they are persuaded there are injustices in a situation. Furthermore, chaplains are expected to become advocates of the constituency they serve. While there are those who believe all chaplains should be supported by their denomination or sending church rather than by the government, the issue at the moment does not seem to be creating much tension and the present system is accepted by an overwhelming majority of the American people.

Patriotism

During the 1988 presidential campaign there was considerable debate as to which candidate was the most "patriotic." Both had served in the military and both had already been in high political office. But the issue of patriotism was raised as an emotional issue and deserves comment from the Christian perspective. There are some who feel that, as Christians, the most patriotic thing to do is simply withdraw from the political process, because it is too filled with compromise and ambiguity. In the past there were conservative religious groups that felt this way. But politics, like all of life, is a battle of hauling and tugging and compromising to get done as much as one can in a world that spins out its existence somewhere east of Eden where perfection is not possible. Nevertheless, there are many (if you consider the large number of voters who do not exercise the franchise) who express their patriotism by standing aside and not being involved.

There are others who feel any criticizing or questioning of government is unpatriotic. United Methodists do not agree with this position any more than we do with the idea that we are to withdraw from participation.

A patriot, from the United Methodist perspective, is one who believes this nation exists *under* God. The Declaration of Independence makes four references to God. Those who framed it said that the Laws of Nature and of Nature's God entitled them to establish a separate nation. They made reference to the fact that persons are endowed by their Creator with certain inalienable rights. They appealed to the Supreme Judge of the world for the rectitude of their intentions, and they concluded with a declaration of reliance on the protection of Divine Providence. When we recite "one nation, under God," we are affirming our conviction that even our nation is under the judgment of Almighty God and our ultimate allegiance is not to country but to our conscience as informed by our faith. Our allegiance to our nation is held under a higher allegiance to the God who is over all the nations. A patriot, therefore, is one who keeps reminding us that we exist by the sufferance of God before whom the generations rise and fall. We are subject to divine correction; we rely upon divine providence.

A Roman Catholic cardinal once said that patriotism should not be a cloak for the blind acceptance of all decisions made by the United States. It is not patriotic to say: "My country, right or wrong." It is patriotic, if I understand the spirit of the framers of the Declaration of Independence, to say: "My country, when it is right, work to keep it right; when it is wrong, make it right again."

The Declaration of Independence affirms that all persons are equal and endowed with certain inalienable rights and closes with the framers mutually pledging to each other their lives, fortunes, and sacred honor. We conclude from this that a patriot is one who takes risks in working for the full dignity of every fellow citizen. America has a split personality. Each day we become richer, yet the chronic poor and homeless multiply. We revere the Constitution and the Declaration of Independence, yet millions seem cordoned off from their full embrace.

One of the important contemporary words is *humanization*. It is not an easy word to define. The best we can do is to suggest that it means helping men and women to become what God intends them to be: not angels, not animals, but humans who know the pleasure of work, the joys of play, the ecstasy of love, and the power of prayer. It is to make it possible for all persons to know justice, to have a fair share of the economic resources of this nation, to accept freedom and responsibility for themselves and others.

The newspaper recently carried an interesting story. When the Mississippi River began to rise, the citizens in Davenport, Iowa, organized to build a dike with sandbags. They called on the high school students to help. There had been trouble in the school with delinquency of all kinds. But during the ten days of the crisis, with many students working night after night, there was not a single disturbance. Mutual responsibility raised them to greatness.

In this there is a lesson for our nation. We are torn by factions. Self-interest groups clamor for what they want. There is a waning of trust in the officials we have elected to represent us. And it appears from the reports we read that "the poor are getting poorer and the rich are getting richer," and this sows the seeds of social unrest. If we can get back to the idea that "all are created equal and endowed with certain inalienable rights" and each of us, all of us, work to assure the fulfillment of this vision, our beloved nation will experience the greatness of which it is capable. Patriotism is everyone working together, building a climate of decency, hope, and opportunity for every citizen.

Epilogue

It is New Year's Day, 1991, more than a year since most of the text for this slender volume was written. As I read newspapers and magazines and listen to CNN, it is obvious that the issues addressed in this book are as relevant now as fifteen months ago.

This is a volatile, complex era, and all of us are searching for workable standards of personal conduct. The social and economic transformations in Europe; the continuing crisis in the Middle East; scandals among political, financial, and even religious leaders; debates over race and human sexuality—all raise questions as to what the guidelines are and should be. It is obvious that ethical choices cannot be left entirely to well-bred instincts, good intentions, and broad principles. Guidelines must be found and stated in sound psychological, social, and religious terms. This is what the Social Principles of The United Methodist Church endeavor to do. And that is why a book such as this, which lifts issues and examines them, which shares the thinking of the church but also leaves room for personal response, can be of value in assisting concerned Christians as they form opinions and ethical guidelines that result in a lifestyle consistent with our deepest religious commitments.

This book was written out of a conviction that our faith must be radically involved in and relevant to the problems, heartaches, tensions, sorrows, and joys of people as we strive to live meaningfully in our uncertain age. Pronouncements and resolutions from church conferences are important and can stimulate our own prayerful thought, but ultimately our task is to find the motivation as individuals to study the Bible and church traditions, as well as sociological and psychological conclusions, and bring all this to bear on the social problems which often confuse God's children. Applying the Christian faith and ethic to the concerns of our time constitutes one of the supreme tasks of all Christians.

Some of the headlines gathered from the media over New Year's weekend illustrate what confronts us. Lester E. (Joe) Cruzan, a United Methodist layman, and his family, won a four-year legal battle that resulted in removal of a feeding tube from his comatose daughter. She died a few days later. The President vetoed the Civil Rights Act of 1990, saying it was a "quota bill." The rise of a former Ku Klux Klan leader in Louisiana to national prominence reminded us that racism is not dead. Newspapers tell us: "We live in a less material world. The color green has more to do with saving the environment than making money." Numerous articles analyze the role of abortion in the 1990 elections. Editorials call out for more laws to stop drunk drivers. Our denomination has a commission that continues to study homosexuality. Conscientious objection to war is again being debated in the press. The issues may be dramatized by new names and different headlines, but their fundamental nature remains unchanged. That is why, in a book such as this, it would be easy to vary the illustrations. They can become "dated." Yet the concerns we are discussing, in their essential nature, continue to challenge us. Reverence for life; regard for truth; respect for environment; human sexuality; marriage and divorce; the ways of peace; a responsible personal lifestyle—issues such as these are ever-present.

In offering this reflection to the church, it is my hope that new members will develop an understanding as to why United Methodists teach and believe as we do; that study groups within the church will find this a useful resource as they struggle to formulate personal guidelines for Christian living; and that pastors will, on occasion, refer to this as a tool in their preparation of sermons.

Christians have always been people of hope. A favorite text of mine is from Paul's affectionate letter to the church at Philippi: "I thank my God in all my remembrance of you . . . thankful for your partnership in the gospel from the first day until now. And I am sure that he who began a good work in you will bring it to completion at the day of Jesus Christ" (1:3-6, RSV).

God is at work. We sing, " . . . though the wrong seems oft so strong, God is the ruler yet." If we believe this, then we must act as people of hope. Give thanks for the battle, that we are to make difficult choices. We have been endowed with dignity and moral responsibility. Nowhere is this more apparent than in the effort to make significant, meaningful, ethical decisions. We will not always agree. United Methodists cherish the right to have diverse opinions. But we commit ourselves to each other in the desire to bring the reign of righteousness here on earth. We pray, "Thy kingdom come, thy will be done, on earth. . . . " Furthermore, each of us has a mandate to say: "And let it begin with me."

EMERSON S. COLAW
January 1, 1991

Endnotes

1. *The Book of Discipline of The United Methodist Church—1988* (Nashville, TN: The United Methodist Publishing House, 1988), p. 91. Used by permission.
2. *Discipline*, p. 92, ¶70.
3. Julian Simon, "Life on Earth Is Getting Better, Not Worse" in *The Futurist* (August 1983). Used by permission of World Future Society.
4. *Discipline*, p. 94, ¶71.
5. Ibid., p. 98, ¶72.
6. Ibid., pp. 94, 95, ¶71.
7. Robert Sinks, "A Theology of Divorce" in *The Christian Century* (April 20, 1977). Copyright © 1977 Christian Century Foundation. Reprinted by permission from the April 20, 1977 issue of *The Christian Century.*
8. "The Revolution Is Over" in *Time* magazine (April 9, 1984). Used by permission.
9. *Discipline*, p. 95, ¶71.
10. Ibid., p. 95, ¶71.
11. Ibid., p. 96, ¶71.
12. Ibid., p. 207, ¶402.
13. Ibid., p. 210, ¶404.
14. Joseph C. Weber, "Reconciliation Rediscovered" in *Manna for the Journey* (now *Open Hands*), Vol. 1, No. 1, P.O. Box 23636, Washington, DC 20026. Used by permission.
15. *The Book of Resolutions of The United Methodist Church, 1988* (Nashville, TN: The United Methodist Publishing House, 1988), p. 120. Used by permission.
16. Frederick Buechner, *Whistling in the Dark* (Harper & Row: 1988), pp. 62, 63. Excerpts from *Whistling in the Dark* by Frederick Buechner. Copyright © 1983 by Frederick Buechner. Reprinted by permission of HarperCollins Publishers.
17. *Resolutions*, p. 101.
18. Merrill McLoughlin, "America's New Civil War," *U.S. News & World Report* (Oct. 3, 1988). Excerpted from Oct. 3, 1988, issue of *U.S. News & World Report.* Used by permission.
19. *Discipline*, p. 96, ¶71.
20. Buechner, p. 1.
21. *Discipline*, p. 97, ¶72.
22. Glenn C. Loury, "A Prescription for Black Progress" in *The Christian Century* (April 30, 1986). Copyright © 1986 Christian Century Foundation. Reprinted by permission from the April 30, 1986, issue of *The Christian Century.*
23. Barbara Reynolds, *USA Today* (Feb. 10, 1989). Copyright © 1989, USA TODAY. Reprinted with permission.
24. Preston Williams, "Remembering King Through His Ideals" in *The Christian Century* (Feb. 19, 1986). Copyright © 1986 Christian Century Foundation. Reprinted by permission from the February 19, 1986, issue of *The Christian Century.*
25. *Discipline*, p. 98, ¶72.
26. Ibid., p. 222, ¶414.
27. Ibid., p. 100, ¶72.

28. Stephen Apthorp, "Drug Abuse and the Church" in *The Christian Century* (Nov. 9, 1988). Copyright © 1988 Christian Century Foundation. Reprinted by permission from the November 9, 1988, issue of *The Christian Century*.
29. Ibid.
30. *Resolutions*, p. 165.
31. *Discipline*, p. 101, ¶72.
32. *Resolutions*, p. 150.
33. *Discipline*, p. 105, ¶74.
34. *The United Methodist Reporter*. Reprinted by permission of *The United Methodist Reporter*, Sept. 2, 1988, editorial.
35. G. A. Studdert-Kennedy, "He Was a Gambler, Too" in *The Unutterable Beauty* (Kent, United Kingdom: Hodder & Stoughton Limited, 1936), p. 117.
36. *Discipline*, p. 107, ¶74.
37. *Resolutions*, pp. 384, 385.
38. Ibid., p. 469.
39. Lloyd Bailey, *Capital Punishment: What the Bible Says* (Nashville, TN: Abingdon, 1987), p. 85.
40. Ibid., p. 91.
41. Marshall Shelley, "Death Penalty: Two Sides of a Growing Issue" in *Christianity Today* (March 2, 1984). Used by permission © *Christianity Today*, 1984.
42. George Boyd, "Capital Punishment: Deserved and Wrong" in *The Christian Century* (Feb. 17, 1988). Copyright © 1988 Christian Century Foundation. Reprinted by permission from the February 17, 1988, issue of *The Christian Century*.
43. *Discipline*, p. 109, ¶75.
44. "Peace on Earth," *USA Today*, Dec. 24, 1987. Copyright © 1987. Reprinted with permission.
45. *Resolutions*, p. 471.
46. Ibid., p. 505.
47. Ibid., p. 525.
48. Ibid., p. 497.
49. *Discipline*, p. 107, ¶74.
50. Jim Wallis, editor, quoting A. J. Muste in *Sojourners* (Vol. 12, No. 5), May 1983, p. 3. Reprinted with permission from *Sojourners*, P.O. Box 29272, Washington, DC 20017.
51. Martin Luther King, Jr., "Letter from Birmingham Jail" in *Why We Can't Wait*. Copyright © 1963, 1964 by Martin Luther King, Jr., copyright © renewed. Reprinted by permission of HarperCollins Publishers Inc.
52. Ibid.
53. L. Harold DeWolf, *Responsible Freedom* (Harper, 1972), p. 315.
54. *Resolutions*, pp. 383, 384.
55. *Discipline*, p. 106, ¶74.